the
Seven
Beggars
& Other
Kabbalistic Tales of
Rebbe Nachman
of Breslov

Translation by **Rabbi Aryeh Kaplan**
Preface by Rabbi Chaim Kramer

JEWISH LIGHTS Publishing

The Seven Beggars:
And Other Kabbalistic Tales of Rebbe Nachman of Breslov

2005 First Printing

Original hardcover edition published by The Breslov Research Institute, Jerusalem/New York.

Library of Congress Cataloging-in-Publication Data
Naòhman, of Bratslav, 1772–1811.
[Sipure ma'asiyot. English. Selections]
The seven beggars and other kabbalistic tales of Rebbe Nachman of Breslov / translation by Aryeh Kaplan ; pref. by Chaim Kramer.
p. cm.
Includes bibliographical references.
ISBN 978-1-58023-250-0 (Pbk.)—ISBN 978-1-68336-435-1 (Hard cover)
1. Hasidic parables. I. Kaplan, Aryeh. II. Title.
BM532.N4213 2005
296.1'9—dc22

2004030903

Manufactured in the United States of America
Cover design: Sara Dismukes

Published by Jewish Lights Publishing
www.jewishlights.com

Contents

To make known and to reveal, that every word that is written in this holy book is Holy of Holies, according to the secrets of the Torah. One shall not think that these are simple stories. For the stories that are in this book were told by the great Tzaddik, Rabbi Nachman of Breslov, may his merit protect us. His intention was to teach us how to serve God. Would it be, that we should understand the great secrets and moral guidance that are in these stories. Then we will be proper Jews, as we should be. May the Almighty send us the Messiah, quickly, in our time, Amen.

RABBI NATHAN OF BRESLOV

Preface

"To separate between the light and the darkness" (Genesis 1:4). The Midrash explains: "The light is a reference to the *ma'asim* of the Tzaddikim, the darkness is a reference to those of the wicked" (*Bereshith Rabbah* 20).

In Hebrew, the word *ma'asim* has a double meaning: deeds and stories.

The teaching of the Midrash is that there are differences as great as the difference between day and night, not only between the deeds of the nations but also between their *stories*.

Our sages knew that in the latter generations the Jews would be exiled and would fall into a profound lethargy.

"And it came to pass that, when the sun was going down, a deep sleep fell upon Abram; and lo, a dread, even a great darkness, fell upon him" (Genesis 15:12).

The sleep, the dread, and the darkness were a vision of the four exiles. The downfall is symbolically represented by the idea of sleep (*Bereshith Rabbah* 44).

There are many who have fallen into this deep sleep. Some people believe they are serving God, but they are really sleeping. The years pass by and what are they left with in the end? There are others who are in such a deep slumber that they do not even know they are asleep (*Likutey Moharan* 60).

The only way to wake people up, Rabbi Nachman tells us, "is through stories."

The Torah is a powerful light which can illumine even the thickest darkness.

Just as a person who has been deprived of light for a long time must not expose himself to glaring sunlight all of a sudden, so too, one who is ignorant of Torah can only be exposed to it in a veiled form at first.

The veil of the Torah is the *ma'asioth,* stories. These stories are a gate which is accessible even to those who are still infinitely far from God. The stories can awaken and revive them.

Our Sages themselves used this method. The Midrash tells us: "When Rabbi Akiva noticed in the course of a lecture that his pupils were getting sleepy, he told them the following story; 'Why did Esther merit to rule over one hundred and twenty-seven provinces?' ..." (*Esther Rabbah* 1). Similarly we find that when Rabbi Yehuda the Prince noticed that his listeners were beginning to get sleepy, he interrupted his lecture and said: "A woman in Egypt gave birth to 600,000 babies!" When his pupils shook themselves out of their drowsiness and asked him what he was talking about, he answered: "It was Yocheved, who gave birth to Moses, who was equal to the 600,000 Jews in Egypt" (*Shir HaShirim Rabbah* 1).

When Rabbi Nachman first started telling his stories, he declared: "Now I am going to tell you stories." The reason he did so was because in generations so far from God the only remedy was to present the secrets of the Torah—including even the greatest of them—in the form of stories. There was no other way to achieve the necessary impact in order to heal us.

Rabbi Nachman was especially concerned that his teachings should be available to all, and this is why he wanted translations in Yiddish and Hebrew.

Breslov Research Institute has undertaken to translate the works of Rabbi Nachman into a number of languages for the benefit of those who are interested in his teachings and stories. The present work is the second in a series of translations of the major works of Rabbi Nachman. It follows "Rabbi Nachman's Wisdom."

There have been a number of translations of Rabbi Nachman's stories. The present work includes a running commentary drawn from the traditional commentaries by Rabbi Nachman's students and followers, giving insight and understanding as to what Rabbi Nachman may have been alluding to. This is the first time that this material has been accessible to the English-speaking reader.

We advise the reader to read through the story first before attempting to study the explanations. The commentary on earlier parts of any given story often contains references to later parts, and without a thorough knowledge of the story itself the reader may not enjoy the full benefits of the commentary.

To achieve a perfect translation without veering from the original by one iota is an impossible task. It is equally impossible to express the exact intention of the author without falling into a laborious literalness. Our intention has been to achieve a translation which is both readable and at the same time sufficiently close to the original that the intention of Rabbi Nachman has been fully conveyed.

Breslov Research Institute wishes to extend its most heartfelt thanks to Rabbi Aryeh Kaplan for this most exacting work. Besides the translation of the stories themselves, collecting and correlating the commentaries from their different sources was a project of monumental difficulty. This will now pave the way for similar work to be done in Hebrew, French, and other languages.

Gratitude is also due to Rabbi Nachman Burstyn and Rabbi Shmuel Moshe Kramer for their valuable assistance in reviewing and editing the manuscripts for publication.

In addition, the Institute hopes to publish other works of Rabbi Nachman in the near future.

May the Almighty accord us the merit of hearing the end of the story, "The Seven Beggars," with the coming of *Mashiach* and the rebuilding of the Holy Temple, Amen.

Chaim Kramer
Founder and Director
Breslov Research Institute
Jerusalem

Translator's Introduction

Rabbi Nachman's stories are among the great classics of Jewish literature. They have been recognized by Jews and non-Jews alike for their
depth and insight into both the human condition and the realm of the
mysterious. As a result, almost a half dozen translations of these stories
have already been made.

When the stories were first published, the book contained both a
Hebrew version and a Yiddish version of the stories. There is some
question as to which was the original, and it may have varied with
different stories. While both versions are essentially the same, minor
variations do crop up, and these have generally been noted.

There is also a huge Breslover literature on the stories that, for the
most part, has been ignored by translators as well as commentators
on the stories. Here, this literature has been gathered together on page
notes to make it readily accessible. Many other allusions to the Bible,
Talmud, Midrash, and Kabbalah are also included in these notes.

It is hoped that these stories will be an inspiration in translation as
they were in the original.

Aryeh Kaplan

Introduction

"Whatever he was, his name has already been given, and it is known that he is Man."

—ECCLESIASTES 6:10

This is the Torah of the holy man[1]—one who was worthy of completing the Form of Man[2]—for this is the entire man.[3]

We are speaking of our glorious master, teacher and rabbi, the crown of our glory,[4] the pride of our strength,[5] the holy, awesome rabbi, the great lamp,[6] the highest lamp, the beautiful, holy lamp—his name is holy—our master and rabbi, the Master, Rabbi Nachman (may the memory of the saint and holy man be a blessing).[7] He was a great-grandson of the holy, awesome, Godly rabbi, the Baal Shem Tov[8] (may the memory of the saint and holy man be a blessing).

1. Paraphrase of Numbers 19:14.

2. See Genesis 1:26, 27. This indicates that Rabbi Nachman was the paradigm of man, and that he was able to perfect the concept of the supernal Man.

3. Ecclesiastes 12:13.

4. cf. Jeremiah 13:18.

5. Leviticus 26:19.

6. See *Zohar* 1:4a.

7. Proverbs 10:7. This expression is used after mentioning the name of a deceased righteous man.

8. Rabbi Israel ben Eliezer (1698–1760) was the founder of the Chassidic movement.

The people Israel have already enjoyed his enlightenment in his holy, wondrous works which have already been published.⁹ Many saw them and rejoiced, and the upright were ecstatic.¹⁰ The truth has shown its own way.¹¹

Now you can see what else is in our pouch. It is a collection of wondrous, awesome tales, which we were worthy of hearing "mouth to mouth"¹² from the Rebbe's holy lips. He perceived, and he pondered and composed many parables.¹³

The Rebbe disguised high and mighty concepts and hid them in his stories in wondrous, awesome ways.

This was the way things were originally done in Israel, through redemption and interchanging.¹⁴ When people wanted to speak of God's hidden mysteries, they would speak in allegory and parable, hiding in many disguises the concealed secrets of the Torah, the King's hidden treasury.

Thus, after telling the story of "The Exchanged Children"¹⁵ the Rebbe said that in ancient times when the Initiates discussed Kabbalah, they would speak in this manner, making use of stories and parables. Until the time of Rabbi Shimon bar Yochai (author of the *Zohar*),¹⁶ they would not openly use explicit Kabbalistic terms.

In most cases, after a number of stories, the Rebbe would reveal some hints to the mysteries alluded to in the story. There would be some allusion as to the significance of the words, but it was very little, less than a drop in the ocean. We will discuss some of these allusions given after the stories in their proper place.

9. The *Sippurey Maasioth* was first published in Ostrog, 1816. The only Breslov works published prior to this were *Likutey Moharan*, Ostrog, 1808, and a second portion, *Likutey Moharan Tinyana*, Mohalov, 1811.

10. From the High Holiday *Amidah.* See Job 22:19.

11. A folk saying. See Ibn Ezra on Proverbs 9:1.

12. Numbers 12:8.

13. Ecclesiastes 12:9.

14. Paraphrase of Ruth 4:7.

15. See p. 245 of *The Lost Princess* (Woodstock, Vt.: Jewish Lights Publishing, 2005).

16. Rabbi Shimon bar Yochai (circa 150 CE) and his disciples were the authors of the *Zohar,* the major classic of Kabbalah.

Until now, we kept these stories in our private files. But many people have said to us, "Why don't you show us this good?"[17] Many members of our group have a deep longing and yearning[18] to be able constantly to hear the words of the Living God[19] that were spoken by our holy rabbi, especially in the stories that he told.

Until now, the stories were not available except in the form of handwritten manuscripts, produced by various scribes. These manuscripts contain so many errors that the main point is often lost. Therefore, people came to us with great yearning, and persuaded us with great longing, until we had no other choice but to fulfill their desire and bring this work to press.

The Rebbe himself also expressed such a desire. Once he declared that he wanted to print the *Sippurey Maasioth,* saying in the presence of many people, "I would like to print the book of stories. It should have the Hebrew written on top, and the Yiddish vernacular on the bottom."

He also once said, "What can people find to complain about this? After all, they are nice stories to tell...." We heard words such as these from his holy lips.

This is what motivated us to bring this work to press. Of course, we are not deluding ourselves, since we realize full well that the Rebbe has had much opposition. However, truth is its own witness.[20] We have an obligation to do God's will, and God will then do as He sees fit.[21] He who wants to listen will listen, and he who wants to refuse will refuse.[22]

Also, thank God, Providence has helped us so that the Rebbe's sacred works have become popular among the holy people. In every congregation in the community of Israel, his words provide the people

17. Psalms 4:7.

18. Psalms 84:3.

19. Jeremiah 23:36.

20. A folk saying. See Rabbi Yosef ibn Caspi, *Adaney Kesef* (London, 1911, Volume 1, p. 66).

21. 2 Samuel, 10:12.

22. Ezekiel 3:27.

with joy and happiness. They are as sweet as honey in their mouths.[23] All of them are satiated and enjoy his good.[24] It is like marrow and fat that satisfies their souls so that with joyous lips, their mouths sing praise.[25]

More people are on our side than are on the side of those who dispute the truth, speaking about the Tzaddik with arrogance, pride and scorn,[26] and making up accusations that are totally unimaginable. We cannot speak at length about this, since it is among God's hidden mysteries. How many worlds are turned upside down because of the disputes that have currently become more prevalent between scholars and tzaddikim? What can be done by a person who comes after the King? What has been done is done.[27]

Nevertheless, we wish to inform everyone that our intent in printing these stories is solely for the sake of members of our group, who wish to find shelter in the Rebbe's holy shadow,[28] yearning, seeking and searching to hear these holy words. The words may be printed in a book, but they are the same as if they had been proclaimed in a great congregation.

Moreover, we see that these stories have already begun to spread in writing through many manuscripts. There is no difference between words in a handwritten manuscript and words in a printed book. Furthermore, the words were never meant to be kept secret.

Whoever has eyes will see, and whoever has a heart will understand. Regarding these stories, it can be said, *It is not an empty thing from you* (Deuteronomy 32:47). As our sages teach, "If it is empty, then it is from you"[29] that is, it is your own fault.

---

23. Ezekiel 3:3.

24. cf. Friday night *Amidah.*

25. Psalms 63:6.

26. Psalms 31:19.

27. Ecclesiastes 2:12.

28. See Judges 9:15; Isaiah 30:2; Psalms 57:2. Rabbi Nathan includes this disclaimer because of the great opposition that he was encountering. A number of Chassidic leaders who felt that they understood these stories claimed that they were too holy for publication.

29. *Yerushalmi, Peah* 1:1; *Zohar* 1:163a.

The words of these stories stand in the highest places. We heard the Rebbe say explicitly that every word of these holy stories has tremendous meaning, and that anyone who changes even a single word of these stories from the way that they were told is taking very much away from the story.

The Rebbe also said that these stories are original concepts (*chidushim*) that are very wondrous and awesome. They contain extraordinary, hidden, deep meanings. They are fit to be preached in public and one may stand in the synagogue and tell any one of these stories. They are extremely lofty, awesome, original concepts.

Moreover, if a person's heart has attained perfection, and he is expert in the sacred works, especially in the books of the *Zohar* and the writings of the Ari,[30] then if he fully concentrates his mind and heart on these stories, he will be able to understand and know a small portion of the allusions found in them.

Also in most places, these stories contain wondrous, highly motivating moral lessons (*mussar*), which an intelligent person can understand by himself. Most of these stories will arouse the heart and draw it very close to God. They will cause a person to repent before God with ultimate sincerity, so that he will dedicate himself fully to Torah and serving God at all times, turning away completely from all worldly vanities. If a person looks at these stories sincerely, he will see this with his mind's eyes.

The ultimate meaning of these stories, however, is far above the grasp of normal human intelligence. It is deep, deep, who can discover it?[31]

It does not pay to praise these stories overmuch, since they are far above our understanding. The more one tries to praise their greatness and depth, the more one takes away from them. The only reason that we have spoken at all was to arouse the hearts of the members of our group, so that they not forget the wonders the Rebbe showed them.

---

30. Rabbi Yitzchak Luria (1534–1572), known as the Ari, was considered one of the greatest Kabbalists of all time. Knowledge of his writings is essential in order to understand much of the Kabbalistic teachings after his time.

31. Ecclesiastes 7:24.

Through the few allusions that he revealed to us after each story, he showed the implication of the words; but still, it was only like seeing gestures from a great distance.[32]

It is true that we have written down some of the allusions that we heard from his holy lips. However, it is obvious to any intelligent person that seeing something in a book is not the same as actually hearing it from the author. This is all the more true of allusions such as these, which are not comprehensible except through such gestures as the movements of the head, winks of the eye, motions of the hand, and the like. Only by seeing these can one begin to understand, and one is even then astounded by what one's eyes have seen. From the distance he will see the greatness of God and His holy Torah, clothed in many garments, as explained in all the sacred texts.

This is how far we can go with a few words, even though they contain very much. Our hearts are still filled with terror; where is the scribe and where is the one who can weigh the outcome?[33] From where will our help come?[34] Who will be moved for us for what has been consumed?[35] Who will stand up for us?

We lift our hearts in our hands to God in heaven.[36] Into His hands we entrust our souls.[37] To You, God, we lift up our souls.[38] Until now, Your mercy has helped us. Help us, for we are depending on You.[39] May God's pleasantness rest upon us,[40] until the Righteous Teacher comes to our community, and our holy, glorious Temple is rebuilt. May

---

32. See *Berakhoth* 46b; *Chagigah* 5b.

33. Isaiah 33:18.

34. Psalms 121:1.

35. The expression used here, *mi yanud,* is found in Isaiah 51:19, Jeremiah 15:5, Nahum 3:7, etc. However, the reading here may be, *mi yagur lanu esh okhelah*—"Who among us shall dwell with the devouring fire?" (Isaiah 33:14).

36. Lamentations 3:41.

37. Psalms 31:6.

38. Psalms 25:1.

39. Daily liturgy.

40. Psalms 90:17.

we look upon Zion, the city of our solemn gatherings;[41] may our eyes behold the King in His glory[42]—quickly, in our days, Amen.

These are my words as writer, typesetter and transcriber, to eat to satisfaction and to cover ancient things.[43]

Signed:

The insignificant Nathan[44] (Reb Noson), son of my father, our rabbi and master, Naftali Hertz[45] (may God protect him and keep him)[46] of Nemerov, and son-in-law of the great rabbi, the saintly one, renowned all over the world. His holy, honorable name is our master, Rabbi David Tzvi[47] (may the memory of the righteous be a blessing in the World to Come), who was head of the rabbinical court in the holy congregation of Kreminetz and its environs, the holy congregation of Sharograd, and the holy congregation of Mohalov and its environs.

Before the Rebbe began telling the story "The Lost Princess" [see *The Lost Princess*], he declared, "Many hidden meanings and lofty concepts are contained in the stories that the world tells. These stories, however, are deficient; they contain many omissions. They are also confused, and people do not tell them in the correct order. What begins the story may be told at the end, and the like. Nevertheless, the folk tales that the world tells contain many lofty hidden mysteries.

41. Isaiah 33:20.

42. Isaiah 33:17.

43. Isaiah 23:18, according to Midrashic interpretation.

44. Rabbi Nathan Sternhartz of Nemerov (1780–1844) was the leading disciple of Rabbi Nachman, and the editor of most of his published works. See above, p. xv.

45. Rabbi Nathan's father, R. Naftali Hertz of Nemerov, was very wealthy, having many stores in Nemerov, Berdichev and Odessa (*Kokhavey Or*, p. 9). Rabbi Nathan's mother was the daughter of Rabbi Yitzchak Danziger (*Avenehah Barzel*, p. 3; *Tovoth Zikhronoth*, p. 13).

46. The abbreviation *NeRU* indicates that Rabbi Nathan's father was alive at this time.

47. Rabbi David Tzvi (ben Aryeh Leib) Ohrbach (died 1808). Rabbi Nathan married his daughter in 1792 (*Yemey Maharnat* 6a. Also see *Avenehah Barzel*, p. 4).

"The Baal Shem Tov (may the memory of a tzaddik and holy man be a blessing) was able to bring about a Unification (*Yichud*)[48] through telling a story. When he saw that the supernal Channels were defective, and it was not possible to rectify them through prayer, he would rectify and unify them by telling stories."

The Rebbe spoke about this. Then he began to tell the story on the following page.[49] He said, "I told this story while on a journey...."[50]

It is important to realize that the stories here are for the most part (if not all) completely new stories that have never before been told. The Rebbe created them with his holy mind, based on the lofty perception that he gained through divine inspiration. He would clothe his perceptions with a particular story, and the story itself would be a demonstration of the awesome, great, lofty perception that he experienced, as well as what he saw in the place that he reached.

The Rebbe would sometimes relate ordinary folk tales, but he would embellish them. He would change the order of the story, so that it was very different than the original folk tale. In this book, however, only one or two such modified folk tales are included. All the other stories are totally new and original.

When the Rebbe (of blessed memory) began telling stories, he said, "I am now beginning to tell stories" (*ich vell shoin an-heiben maasios der-tzeilen*). His intent was as if to say, "I must tell stories because my lessons and conversations are not having any effect in bringing you back to God." All his life, he made great effort to bring us close to God, but when all this did not help, he began to engage in telling stories.

It was around this time[51] that the Rebbe taught the lesson that

---

48. A *Yichud* is the unification of two spiritual forces that have been separated.

49. In the first edition, there was no second introduction, so the stories began on the page after the introduction.

50. See p. 1 of *The Lost Princess*.

51. This lesson was said on Rosh HaShanah, 5567 (1806), about two or three weeks after the first story was told (*Yemey Moharnat* 12a; *Chayay Moharan* 34a #11, 22b #14). See note p. 1 of *The Lost Princess*.

begins, "Rabbi Shimon said, 'It is a time to do for God, they have disregarded Your Torah'" (Psalms 119:126)....[52] This is speaking of the Torah of the Ancient One...[53] It is printed in the first book on page 157.[54]

At the end of this lesson, the Rebbe speaks a bit about stories. He says that people may be asleep all their lives, but through stories told by a true tzaddik, they can be awakened.... See what is written there.[55]

There are some stories that are "in the midst of years."[56] However, there are other stories from ancient times that are included in the concept of the Ancient One.[57] If you study the entire lesson well, you will have some awareness and understanding as to the lofty implications of these stories as well as the Rebbe's holy intent in telling them.

In most cases, even the plain, simple meaning of these stories can strongly motivate a person toward God. All these stories consist of awesome mysteries, but aside from their secret meanings, they have great power to motivate everyone toward God. Be strong.

Rabbi Nathan of Breslov, 1816

52. *Likutey Moharan* 60. The quotation here, which opens the lesson, is from the *Zohar* 3:128a.

53. In Aramaic this is Atik (see Daniel 7:9, 13, 22), which is the highest of the supernal *partzufim* or persona.

54. In the first edition of *Likutey Moharan*, Ostrog, 1808.

55. *Likutey Moharan* 60:6.

56. Ibid., from Habakkuk 3:2. This is a story that is obviously related to a Torah lesson.

57. See note 53.

1   The Seven Beggars*

I will tell you how people once rejoiced.*

The Seven Beggars. The first story in this volume, "The Seven Beggars" is actually story number thirteen of Rebbe Nachman's famous tales. See *The Lost Princess* (Woodstock, Vt.: Jewish Lights Publishing, 2005) for the first twelve of his famous stories.

This story was begun on a Friday night (March 30, 1810) and was told in parts during the following week (*Chayay Moharan* 15c 49; *Yemey Moharnat* 31b). See next note.

That Friday night, Rabbi Nachman told the first part of the story until the end of the first day after the wedding, where the blind beggar tells his story. Rabbi Nathan was home in Nemerov when the story was told. However, the next Tuesday, his friend, Reb Naftali (see *Yemey Moharnat* 31b), came to his house and repeated the story. Rabbi Nathan was so astounded that he just stood there trembling. He had heard many stories from Rabbi Nachman, but he had never heard anything like that. He went to Breslov that evening, but Rabbi Nachman was already sleeping. The next day, Wednesday (April 4), Rabbi Nachman outlined the entire story and explained the subplot where each one remembers back as far as he can. This was interrupted when Rabbi Nachman's attendant, Reb Michel (see *Yemey Moharnat* 21b), came in and told them it was time for his meal (*Sichoth HaRan* 149).

As with many lessons and stories, this one began with a mundane discussion, "an awakening from below." Rabbi Nathan reviewed the story with others, but Rabbi Nachman's introductory remarks to the story were lost (*Sichoth HaRan* 151).

Rabbi Nachman himself held that this story was very great. He said, "If I only told the world this one story, I would still be truly great" (*Likutey Halakhoth, Tefillin* 5:1; see end of story). He said that this story could be used as a sermon in synagogue (*Chayay Moharan* 16b 4).

I will tell you... The story happened to be told because one of Rabbi Nachman's followers had sent him a snuff box. Rabbi Nathan wrote one of his friends about it and told him to remain happy. When Rabbi Nachman saw this letter, he said, "I will tell you how people once rejoiced," and with that, he began the story (*Sichoth HaRan* 149).

According to some sources, Rabbi Nachman's actual words here were, "Since you are so depressed, what do you know about being happy? I will tell you how people once rejoiced" (*Chayay Moharan* 16b 4). According to another source, he said, "I will tell you how, out of depression, people were able to rejoice" (*Chokhmah U'Tevunah* 15:1).

There was once a king* who had an only son.* The king wanted to give over his kingdom* to his son during his lifetime.

On the day of his son's coronation, the king made a great ball.* Whenever the king makes a ball, there is great rejoicing. But now, when the king was giving over the kingdom to his son during his lifetime, the rejoicing was immense. All the royal ministers, dukes* and officials were there, and they rejoiced greatly at this feast.

Everyone in the land was also pleased* by this. It was a great historic event* that the king was giving the kingdom over to his son during his lifetime, and there was great rejoicing. There were all sorts of entertainment at the ball, such as bands,* comedians,* and the like; everything to make people rejoice.*

king. God.

only son. Israel. It is thus written, "My son, my firstborn, is Israel" (Exodus 4:22). In a more general sense, however, this refers to mankind as a whole.

give over his kingdom. God thus gave all dominance to Israel and the righteous. It is thus written that God said, "I will say to Zion, you are My people (*ami*)" (Isaiah 51:16). The *Zohar* says, "Do not read *ami*—'My people'—but *imi* 'with Me' so that the verse would read, 'I will say to Zion, you are with Me.'" This indicates that the Israelites are God's partners in sustaining and directing the world (*Zohar* 1:5a).

It is possible to say that this occurred with the giving of the Torah, where God promised the Israelites that they would be a "Kingdom of Priests" (Exodus 19:6). This was a time of great rejoicing, as we say in the *Piut* for Shavuoth, "Those on high rejoiced, and those below exulted, when the Torah was received at Sinai."

If we say that the son is mankind as a whole, then this "giving over of power" denotes the creation of the physical world.

The concept of a king giving his son his kingdom during his lifetime is paralleled by King David, who gave his throne to Solomon (see 1 Kings 2; *Oneg Shabbath*, p. 31).

ball. The Yiddish word *bal* is used. Rabbi Nachman taught that there was a concept of dancing when the Torah was given (see *Sichoth HaRan* 86).

dukes. *Dukhsin* in Yiddish.

pleased. The word here is *hana'eh*, which denotes pleasure, but also denotes benefit. It can be translated either way.

historic event. Literally, "honor."

bands. *Kapelesh*.

comedians. *Kamediesh*. See "The Humble King" and "The Spider and the Fly" (in *The Lost Princess*).

When the rejoicing reached its peak, the king stood up and said to his son, "I am an expert in astrology, and I see that you are destined to lose your kingdom. When you lose power, be careful not to become depressed; you must remain joyful.* If you are happy, then I will also be happy. But if you become sad, then I will still be happy—because you are no longer king. If you are not able to remain happy when you lose your royal power, then you are not fit to be a king. But if you remain happy, then I will be extremely happy."

The king's son took over the kingdom with a firm hand.* He appointed his own ministers, dukes and officials, and set up his own army.*

The king's son was very wise, and he loved wisdom* very much. He surrounded himself with great sages. Whenever anyone presented him with a wise thought, he cherished it, and gave the person whatever he

rejoice. There is always rejoicing in God's presence, especially when He is being honored. It is thus written, "Honor and majesty are before Him, strength and joy are in His place" (1 Chronicles, 16:27).

This great, lavish ball at the beginning of the story is to be contrasted with the poor conditions of the children's wedding later. Nevertheless, the joy was the same on both occasions.

remain joyful. The lesson is that even if one falls, one must remain happy. If a person allows himself to become depressed, then he deserves his downfall (*Rimzey Maasioth*).

Furthermore, whenever a person falls, it is for the sake of ultimately elevating him further (*Oneg Shabbath*, p. 301). Therefore, when a person remains happy even when he falls, he will eventually reach this higher level (ibid. p. 31).

Here the king told his son to be happy. Later in the story, the beggars make the children happy at their wedding.

firm hand. *Yad ramah* in Hebrew. This means "high-handedly" (see Exodus 14:9). In Yiddish, the expression used is *zehr sharf*, which literally means "very sharp," but idiomatically means "in a very strong manner."

army. He had all the symbols of power, but he became so engrossed in sophistry that he forgot how to use them.

wisdom. Sophistry rather than true wisdom. *Chokhmoth* in Hebrew, which often denotes secular wisdom or mental gymnastics. This was very much like the "wisdom" in the story of "The Sophisticate and the Simpleton" (see *The Lost Princess*).

This might be an allegory of Adam, who "loved wisdom" and hence ate from the Tree of Knowledge. As a result, he forgot the art of war—against evil (see below p. 4).

wanted, whether honor or wealth.* If the person wanted wealth he would be given wealth; if he wanted honor, he would be given honor. The king's son valued wisdom so much, he would give anything for it.

All the people therefore became involved in academic studies. Soon the entire land was involved with wise thoughts. Those who desired wealth did so to receive wealth from the king's son, while others did it to gain importance and honor.

Since everyone was immersed in theoretical studies, the land forgot the art of war.* The people became so totally involved in mental gymnastics, that they all became very intelligent, even the least of them. The people developed such high intelligence that the least of them would be the most intelligent people in other lands. The wise men of that land were therefore extremely intelligent.

As a result of their secular studies, the wise men of that land became atheists.* They convinced the king's son of their ideas, and he also became an atheist.

The common people, however, did not become atheists. The arguments of the wise men were so deep and subtle* that the common people could not grasp them, and therefore they were not harmed by these ideas. But the king's son and the wise men all became atheists.

Nevertheless, the king's son had a spark of good in him. He had been born with good, and he had a good nature. Whenever he contemplated his situation, and realized what he was doing ... he would moan and sigh* because he had fallen into such confused beliefs.

---

honor or wealth. The secular world promises honor and wealth. Actually, however, honor and wealth come from God (1 Chronicles, 29:12). The main source of honor and wealth is the Torah (Proverbs 3:16, 8:18, 22:4; cf. Ecclesiastes 6:2).

forgot the art of war. The people forgot how to fight against evil (Likutey Etzoth B, Chakirah 4).

atheists. Nithpaker in Hebrew, but "became apikorsim" in the Yiddish.

The lesson is that even a great person must be very careful not to be led astray by his intellect. In this land, the people became atheists because of their highly developed intellects (Rimzey Maasioth). Secular studies often lead a person away from true belief (Likutey Etzoth B, Chakirah 4).

deep and subtle. Dakuth in Hebrew.

moan and sigh. Even when a person falls away from faith, sometimes he remembers who

Realizing that he had fallen into error, he would moan and sigh very much. But then he would try to think logically,* and he would once again become immersed in his atheistic ideas. This happened many times. When he contemplated, he would moan and sigh, but as soon as he began to think logically, his atheistic ideas would overwhelm him.*

One day* there was a mass flight* from a certain country. All the people fled, and in the course of their flight, they passed through a forest. There, a boy and girl* were lost.* One person lost a little boy, and another lost a little girl. They were both small children, around four or five years old.*

he is (*Rimzey Maasioth*). In general, a Jew might become weak in belief, but there are times when he doubts his own disbelief.

try to think logically. This is because there are systems of thought that can totally confuse a person's logic. One's logic depends completely on the system of axioms that one accepts initially.

Regarding such use of the intellect it is written, "Do not be overly wise" (Ecclesiastes 7:16) (*Rimzey Maasioth*).

would overwhelm him. This part of the story seems to break off abruptly, and it is not brought to a conclusion (*Rimzey Maasioth*; also see end of story). However, it may be related to the story of the beggar without feet (see below; *Chokhmah U'Tevunah* 15:1). Then, just as the handless beggar healed the king's daughter, the footless one healed the king's son who had lost his faith (ibid.).

One day. Literally, "A day came." (See "The King and the Emperor" in *The Lost Princess.*) This may also indicate that this is a continuation of the previous part of the story (*Chokhmah U'Tevunah* 15:1).

mass flight. *Berichah* in Hebrew. Some say that this relates to the king's land. They were exiled because they could not fight (Rabbi Rosenfeld).

This mass flight may refer to the Great Flood, the scattering of people after the Tower of Babel, or the exile of Israel. It may also denote the breaking of the vessels.

boy and girl. *Zakhar* and *nekevah*; literally, "a male and a female." The two children can represent Israel and the Shekhinah, or alternatively, the body and the soul.

were lost. When people flee from the true purpose in life, sensitive people are lost.

four or five years old. Above this, a child is considered to have enough intellect to engage in monetary transactions (*Gittin* 59a).

The children did not have any food.* They began to scream and weep because they did not have anything to eat.

Suddenly a beggar* appeared. He had a sack* in which he was carrying bread. The children approached him and began to follow him. He gave them some bread and they ate.

"How did you come to be here?" he asked them.

"We don't know," they replied. They were only little children.

When he began to leave, they asked him to take them along. "I do not want* you to go with me," he replied.

Meanwhile they got a better look at him, and they realized that he was blind.* They found this very surprising. If he was blind, how did he find his way? Actually, it might seem strange that they were surprised at this, since they were still little children. But they were very intelligent children, and therefore found this surprising.

The blind beggar blessed them* that they should be like him, saying that they should be old like him. He left them some bread to eat and he went on his way. The children realized that God was watching over them, and had brought them this blind beggar to give them food.

did not have any food. Perhaps they were as hungry for spiritual food as for material food.

beggar. The beggars are the main characters in the story. The great tzaddikim are called beggars, since they seem very insignificant in the eyes of the world. The light of great tzaddikim is hidden so much that they appear to be totally disabled (*Likutey Etzoth* B, Tzaddik 97). Furthermore, they are called beggars because they were worthy of this great level only because they begged God to help them. Rabbi Nachman thus taught that all tzaddikim attained their achievements primarily through prayer (*Rimzey Maasioth*, note at end).

The Yiddish word used for beggar is *betler*, which also means "seeker."

sack. *Tarbas* in Yiddish.

I do not want. Perhaps because they had to meet the other six beggars. Moreover, they would not be worthy of following in his path until they were married.

blind. The seven beggars represent the seven leaders of Israel: Abraham, Isaac, Jacob, Moses, Aaron, Joseph, and David. Some say that the blind one represented Isaac, who was blind (Genesis 27:1). The blind beggar also represents the first day of creation, when light was made.

blessed them. Each day a beggar gave them a different blessing. The concept of a different blessing each day is related to the verse, "Bless God each day" (Psalms 68:20) (*Nachath HaShulchan, Yoreh Deah* 242, p. 47a).

When the bread was used up, they began to cry for food again. Night fell and they slept. In the morning, they did not have anything to eat, and they cried out and wept.

Meanwhile, another beggar came. They realized that he was deaf.* As soon as they began to speak to him, he made gestures with his hands indicating that he did not hear. He also gave them some bread. When he was about to leave, they asked him to take them along, but he refused. He also blessed them that they should be like him. With that, he left them some bread and went on his way.

When the bread was used up, they cried out again. Another beggar appeared, and he had a speech defect.* When they began to speak to him, he stammered* so badly that they could not understand what he was saying. He could understand them, but because of his stammering, they could not make out what he was saying. He also gave them bread, and before he left, blessed them that they should be like him. He then went on his way, just as the previous ones had.

Later, another beggar came. He had a crooked neck.* The same thing happened as before.

Then another beggar came, and he was a hunchback.*

Later, a beggar without hands* came.

Finally, they encountered a beggar without feet.*

---

deaf. Some say that he represents Abraham. There is a Midrash that speaks of Abraham as "God's deaf servant."

speech defect. *Kaved peh* in Hebrew; literally, "heavy of mouth." The Torah speaks of Moses as being *kevad peh* (Exodus 4:10).

stammered. *Megamgem* in Hebrew; *Geshamperet* in Yiddish.

crooked neck. Some say that this is Aaron, who was able to enter the Holy of Holies.

hunchback. *Hokir* in Yiddish. Some say that this is Jacob. He is the pillar who supports the world.

without hands. Some say that this is Joseph, representing the tzaddik, who can rectify the *brit*.

without feet. Some say that this is David. Regarding Malkhuth it is written, David is Malkhuth, and "Her feet go down to death" (Proverbs 5:5).

There is no definite tradition as to which beggar may represent which leader. At the end of the story, however, Rabbi Nachman himself relates King David to the third day.

Each one of these beggars gave them bread, and blessed them that they should be like him. Each one behaved in the same manner.

When all their bread was used up, they began to walk, hoping to come to an inhabited area. They came to a path and followed it until they came to a small town. The children came to a house, and the people had pity on them, and gave them some bread. They went to another house, and the people also gave them food. They thus began to go from door to door. The children realized that things were going well for them, and that people were giving them bread.*

The children promised each other that they would always remain together. They made themselves large beggars' sacks,* and continued going from door to door.* They also attended all celebrations, such as circumcision ceremonies and weddings.

They then decided to move on, and they went to the larger cities, where they also begged from door to door. They went to the fairs, where they sat together with the other beggars by the fences,* holding their alms plate.

Eventually, these children became well known to all the beggars. They all knew them, and were aware that they were the children who had been lost in the forest.

Once there was a huge fair in one of the large cities. All the beggars went there, and these children were also there. Suddenly the beggars got the idea that these two children would be a perfect match for one another, and that they should be married. As soon as a few of the beg-

---

The seven beggars represent the entire human structure, from head to foot. As we shall see, these beggars were so perfect that, to an imperfect world, they appeared to be disabled (*Rimzey Maasioth*).

As mentioned earlier, the seven beggars, in a sense, denote the "seven shepherds." However, Rabbi Nathan said, that since Rabbi Nachman knew these praises, he must have attained these levels himself (*Yemey Moharnat* 44b, 45a).

and that people... In Yiddish but not in Hebrew.

beggars' sacks. *Tarbas* in Yiddish.

from door to door. The beggars all blessed the children that they should be like them, and one benefit that the children derived from this was that they learned to be beggars.

fences. *Prezbes* in Yiddish.

gars began to discuss it, they all agreed that it was an excellent idea, and the match was made. The only problem was how to make a wedding.

When they discussed the problem, they realized that soon it would be the king's birthday, and that he was making a public feast.* All the beggars decided to go there, and any meat and bread that they could beg would be used to make the wedding.

The beggars carried out their plan and went to the public feast. All the beggars went to the feast, and they begged meat and bread. They also gathered the meat and fine white bread* that was left over from the feast.

They then went and dug a huge pit, large enough to hold one hundred men. They covered it with reeds, earth and dung.* All of them then entered the pit, and they made a wedding* for the children. The beggars brought them under the marriage canopy* and were very, very joyous.*

public feast. *Minyanes* in Yiddish.

fine white bread. *Kolitch* in Yiddish.

reeds, earth, and dung. The reeds are reminiscent of the covering on a sukkah. However, the dirt and dung are to camouflage the place. When something very holy is done, it sometimes must be camouflaged so that the forces of evil will not deter it. The dirt and dung covering the hole might represent the physical world. It is also possible that the reeds, dirt, and dung represent the three *klipoth*.

It is significant that the beggars only reveal themselves in this pit covered with dung. The true greatness of a tzaddik can only be seen in the physical world (*Likutey Etzoth* B, *Tzaddik* 97).

wedding. The wedding refers to the Messianic age, when there will be a full joining between God (the Bridegroom) and the Shekhinah (the Bride). Alternatively, this can be an allusion to the Giving of the Torah, which the Talmud likens to a wedding (*Taanith* 31a). Actually, if the Israelites had not sinned with the Golden Calf, the Giving of the Torah would have been the final rectification (*Avodah Zarah* 3a).

The lowly state of this wedding can be contrasted with the great pomp in the hall at the beginning of the story. In both cases there was great joy. But the ball at the beginning denoted the joy at creation, while here the joy is because of the rectification of a very imperfect world.

marriage canopy. *Chupah* in Hebrew. This symbolizes the bride and groom entering into one household. The Midrash states that at the Giving of the Torah, God held Mount Sinai over the Israelites like a marriage canopy (*Rokeach* 353).

joyous. Just as the king told his son to be happy, so the beggars now made the couple happy. The first was a case of "awakening from above," while this may be a case of "awakening from below."

The bridegroom and bride were also extremely joyous. They began to remember the kindness* that God had shown them when they were in the forest. They wept and yearned* very much, saying, "If only the first beggar—the blind one—who had brought us bread in the forest—could be here."

The First Day

Suddenly, while they were yearning very greatly for the blind beggar,* he spoke up and said: Here I am! I've come to be at your wedding. I am giving you a wedding present* that you should be old like me. I originally gave you this as a blessing,* but now I am giving this as a full gift for your wedding present—that you should have a long life like mine.

You think that I am blind. Actually, I am not blind at all.* But the

---

remember the kindness. When a person experiences a time of joy, he should remember all the good that God has done for him and thank God for it (*Rimzey Maasioth*).

yearned. Because of their yearning for the blind beggar, he came to the wedding. From here we see the power of yearning and longing (see *Likutey Moharan* 31). We also see the level of these children, who could bring about things through their yearning alone (*Rimzey Maasioth*).

Furthermore, they actually mentioned the blind beggar. When a person mentions the name of a tzaddik, he becomes bound to that tzaddik (see *Sefer HaMiddoth, Tzaddik* II, 20). It is for this reason that, when the children mentioned the blind beggar, he came to them (*Chayay Nefesh* 48).

blind beggar. See above.

wedding present. *Matanah liDerashah* in Hebrew; *drasha geshank* in Yiddish. It is a custom for the bridegroom to give a discourse (*derashah*) at his wedding, and the gifts are seen as being given, not for the wedding, but for the discourse. Therefore, they are called *drasha geshank*, or "discourse gifts" (see *Sichoth HaRan*).

blessing. Marriage is an extremely high concept. When a couple is married, they can produce a child, thus bringing down a soul from the highest realms. The source of souls is the Divine itself, higher than all four supernal universes (see *Likutey Moharan* 17). It is for this reason that the seven beggars blessed the couple when they became married (*Likutey Halakhoth, Tefillath Minchah* 7:93).

I am not blind... Both he and the deaf beggar are alluded to in the Messianic prophecy, "Who is blind, except for My servant, and deaf like the messenger I send? Who is blind like the perfect one, blind like God's servant? Seeing many things, you do not watch it, and opening the ears of the deaf, he will not hear" (Isaiah 42:19,20).

entire duration* of the world's existence is not considered by me to be even like the blink of an eye.

(It was for this reason that he appeared to be blind; he did not look at the world* at all. Since the entire duration of the world's existence was not considered by him to be even like the blink of an eye,* the entire concept of looking* at anything in the world or seeing it did not apply to him at all.)

I am extremely old,* but I am completely young.* I have not yet begun to live, but nevertheless, I am very old.

the entire duration. This phrase is only in the Hebrew, but not in the Yiddish. Therefore, the Yiddish would be translated, "All the world's existence is not considered to be like the blink of an eye." The beggar is saying that he has such an extended concept of time, that the entire duration of the universe's existence is like no more than an eyeblink to him.

did not look at the world. The true tzaddik does not derive any enjoyment whatsoever from the world. On the highest level, he only wants to please God and does not want even the rewards of the Future World. This is the level of the blind beggar, who did not want even to look at the world (*Likutey Halakhoth, Yoreh Deah, Shiluach HaKen* 4:11, p. 134a).

like the blink of an eye. The blind beggar boasts of his long life. Here we see that his life is so long, that even the duration of the world's existence is like nothing compared to it. Since the duration of the world's existence is like nothing to him, he does not look at the world, and therefore appears to be blind (*Likutey Etzoth* B, *Tzaddik* 88).

In many ways, the blind beggar is like a person who is sleeping. All of time is for him like an instant, and he does not see (*Parparoth LeChokhmah, Eruvin* 65; see *Likutey Moharan Tinyana* 7; see *Chokhmah U'Tevunah* 16).

concept of looking. If a person watches his sight, then he is not susceptible to the Evil Eye and will have an unusually good memory (see *Likutey Moharan* 54:1). Furthermore, if a person does not look at this world, and always keeps the World to Come in mind, he will also have a great memory. This was the level of the blind beggar (*Likutey Halakhoth, Birkath HaRiyah* 5:8). The blind beggar is thus blind primarily because he is aware that the entire world is nothing more than an illusion.

I am extremely old. This was the level of Isaac, regarding whom it is written, "When Isaac was old, his eyes were dim, so that he could not see" (Genesis 27:1).

Once Rabbi Nachman said, "I am the oldest of the old." It was understood that he was referring to the level of the blind beggar (*Shevachey Moharan* 7a 32).

completely young. On a simple level, this means that he is always beginning to serve God anew. Since one is always making a new beginning, it is as if one's life were just starting. God thus speaks of the commandments "that I command you today" (Deuteronomy 6:6), and the sages teach, "The Torah should always be like something brand new" (*Sifri*). Likewise, Moses told the Israelites, "Listen, Israel, today you are becoming a people to God your Lord" (Deuteronomy 27:9). Rashi comments that this means that one's serving God should always be as if one were starting "today" (*Likutey Halakhoth, Tefillin* 5:5).

Furthermore, God is constantly renewing creation. According to the creation of this instant, then, one has actually not yet begun to serve God. Furthermore, the Ari teaches that every second is completely different, and no one second is like any one that ever existed (*Etz Chaim, Drush Egolim VeYosher* 5). Moreover, when a person makes each day holier than the previous one, he is accomplishing more on that day, and the day thus becomes "longer." This is the mystery of "length of days" (*Likutey Moharan* 60). In order to accomplish this, one must forget everything that he did in previously serving God, and begin anew (*Likutey Halakhoth*, loc. cit.; *Likutey Etzoth* B, *Tzaddik* 88).

The Evil One is called an "old and foolish king" (Ecclesiastes 4, see *Likutey Moharan* 1). He is given this name because the foolishness that he teaches people is that one is old and weak and cannot change any more. But here we see that true old age is being able to look at life as if it were just beginning (*Likutey Halakhoth, Tefillin* 5:6).

Thus, we can learn from the blind beggar the power of this continuous renewal. One must be blind when it comes to looking at obstacles in one's path to serving God (*Likutey Halakhoth, Tefillin* 5:9).

God said to the Messiah, "I have given birth to you today" (Psalms 2:7). The Messiah will thus be seen as a newborn babe. Yet at the same time, it is taught that the soul of the Messiah existed from the very beginning of creation (*Likutey Halakhoth, Tefillin* 5:15).

King David, the ancestor of the Messiah, was therefore likened to the moon. The moon is the paradigm of this concept, since it is very old, yet constantly being renewed. The Israelites are also likened to the moon (Song of Songs 7:3). Likewise, the Israelites establish their calendar according to the moon. This is because we must be constantly renewed like the moon (*Likutey Halakhoth, Tefillin* 5:18,19).

This is also the basic concept of the cycles of the month and the year (see *Likutey Moharan Tinyana* 1). Rosh HaShanah is therefore called the "Day of Remembrance" (*Yom HaZikaron*). The blind one, who had perfected the concept of renewal, also had the greatest memory. He was able to reach the highest level of renewal, which is the root of memory (*Likutey Halakhoth, Tefillin* 5:23,24).

Moses thus told the Israelites, "You, who are attached to God, are all alive *today*" (Deuteronomy 4:4). When a person is truly attached to God, then he is in a constant state of renewal, just as God is constantly renewing creation. Then his life is just beginning "today" (*Likutey Halakhoth, Tefillin* 5:25).

If Adam had not sinned, he would have been included, to the greatest possible extent, in the Infinite Being (*Ain Sof*). Of course, he could not have kept contact with *Ain Sof*, but he would have touched it for the most infinitesimal instant, this being the concept of "running and returning" (Ezekiel 1:14). He would then have been infinitely old and infinitely young, just like the blind beggar (*Likutey Halakhoth, Tefillin* 5:18).

Kabbalistically, this is the level of Kether. Kether is the first and oldest of the sefiroth, yet it is before time and, thus, has not yet begun to exist. Thus, the Divine Name associated with Kether is *Ehyeh*, which means, "I will be" (Exodus 3:14). This is the level where being has not yet begun. It is the concept of being in a state of pregnancy, where one can only say, "I will be," and not "I am." God revealed this name to Moses just

This is not merely my own opinion; I also have the word* of the
Great Eagle.* Let me tell you the story:*

before the Exodus, which was the birth of Israel (*Likutey Halakhoth, Tefillin* 5:26; cf.
Likutey Moharan 6).

The Exodus is seen as a concept of birth (Ezekiel 16:5). Similarly, the final redemption is
also a concept of birth, as it is written, "Zion shall give birth to her children" (Isaiah 66:8)
(*Likutey Halakhoth, Tefillin* 5:29).

The redemption, again, can only be brought about through repentance. This is the
concept of beginning anew, and particularly, a new start each day. This is the concept
of the youth of the blind beggar (*Likutey Halakhoth, Tefillin* 5:32).

If the seven beggars are seen as paralleling the seven lower sefiroth, then the blind
beggar would parallel the sefirah of Chesed, as well as the first day of creation. This is
logical, because on the first day light was created, but it was a light that was stored away
for the righteous in the World to Come, and not a worldly light. Hence, one who saw
with this light would be blind to everything worldly.

It is significant to note that in the story "The Master of Prayer" (see *The Lost Princess*),
the sefirah of Chesed is also apparently represented by a child.

word. *Haskamah* in Hebrew. The word means agreement or approbation.

Great Eagle. The obvious allusion here is to the verse, "God satisfied your old age with good
things, so that your youth is renewed like the eagle" (Psalms 103:5). Rashi comments on
this that an eagle becomes younger the older it gets. As we shall see, just like the blind
beggar, the Eagle is also very old, yet very young (*Likutey Halakhoth, Tefillin* 5:5).

The Eagle, of course, was one of the animals that Ezekiel saw in the *merkavah* (Ezekiel
1:10). It is taught that of these animals, the lion represents the Messiah son of David, the
ox represents the Messiah son of Joseph, and the eagle represents Elijah (*Reshith
Chokhmah, Chupath Eliahu*). Thus the animals in the *merkavah* represent the person-
ages involved in the redemption. It is also taught that Divine Inspiration (*ruach
hakodesh*) brings Elijah. Elijah brings the resurrection (*Avodah Zarah* 20b). Thus, it is
Elijah who tells the people to go back to their bodies (*Chokhmah U'Tevunah* 16).

Others, however, say that the Eagle here represents God Himself, as it is written, "As
an eagle stirs up its nest ... so God led them..." (Deuteronomy 32:11,12). It is also taught
that one of the keys that God never gave to another is the key to resurrection (*Taanith*
2a) (*Chokhmah U'Tevunah* 16, in note).

Other sources say that the Great Eagle is the angel in charge of the resurrection. This is
also apparent later from the story (*Rimzey Maasioth*).

Later we see that the Eagle also said that it "was very old but very young." This might
be alluded to in the verse, "I was young, and I have also become old" (Psalms 37:25).
The Talmud states that this verse was said by the angel Metatron (*Yebamoth* 16a). The
Zohar, however, also says that Metatron is the angel in charge of the resurrection (*Zohar*
1:181b; *Rimzey Maasioth*).

the story. The story of the elders is a story from "ancient times," that is, from another
plane of reality (cf. *Likutey Moharan* 60; *Likutey Halakhoth, Tefillin* 5:18). The first

Once upon a time, people took to the sea* in many ships.* A great storm came, and shattered the ships.* The people, however, survived, and they came to a tower. They went up into the tower,* and there they found food, drink, clothing,* and everything else that they needed. All good things, and every pleasure in the world was there.

The people began to converse, and they decided that each one should tell an ancient story involving his earliest memory.* Each one

generations after Adam were an aspect of Arikh Anpin, and all the events that happened then were stories from "ancient times" (*Likutey Halakhoth, Tefillin* 5:21).

people took to the sea. These were the souls of the righteous, who came down to the world (*Rimzey Maasioth*).

ships. The story later states explicitly that these ships are the bodies. The *Zohar* also speaks of the ship that carried Jonah as being an allusion to the body that serves as a vehicle for the soul (*Zohar* 2:199a; *Rimzey Maasioth*).

shattered the ships. This is death, where the body is shattered (*Rimzey Maasioth*; cf. *Zohar* 2:199a).

tower. This is the world of souls, where souls remain until the time of the resurrection (*Rimzey Maasioth* see *Derekh HaShem* 1:3,11,12). The tower is reminiscent of the Pearl Castle in "The Lost Princess" (see *The Lost Princess*).

food, drink, clothing. Food in the Future World is Torah, while clothing is good deeds (*Sichoth HaRan* 23).

earliest memory. This is not simple memory, but the memory of souls involving the highest levels of creation (cf. *Rimzey Maasioth*). All of these tzaddikim were boasting about the supernal worlds. Each one boasted about what he had gained in an upper world (*Likutey Halakhoth, Tefillin* 5:1).

Rabbi Nathan teaches that this entire episode involves tefillin, since tefillin are an aspect of memory, as it is written, "They shall be a sign on your hand, and a memory device (*zikaron*) between your eyes" (Exodus 13:9). The Torah specifically says, "between your eyes," because as we see in this story, memory depends on the rectification of the eyes. Thus, the blind beggar ended up having the best memory of all. Elsewhere, Rabbi Nachman also teaches that memory depends on the eyes (*Likutey Moharan* 54; *Likutey Halakhoth, Tefillin* 5:3).

Thus, the eight old men here represent the eight sections (*parshioth*) in the tefillin, four in the head tefillin, and four in the hand tefillin (ibid.).

Tefillin are related to the eight sections of Aaron's beard. These are the source of the eight writings. This is the holiness of old age (ibid.).

Memories such as these are also found in the Talmud. A number of Talmudic sages remembered events surrounding their births (*Yerushalmi, Kethuboth* 5; *Likutey Halakhoth, Tefillin* 5:45, end; *Rimzey Maasioth*).

would tell what he remembered from the time that his memory began.

There were old and young people present. They honored the oldest man among them to tell his story first.

"What shall I tell you?" he said. "I can even remember when they cut the apple from the branch."*

No one understood what he meant. However, there were wise men there, and they said, "This is obviously a very ancient story."

They then honored the second one to tell his story. The second one, who was not as old as the first, said, "Is that then an old story?* That story I also remember! But I can also remember when the lamp* was lit!"

"This story is even older than the first!" said the wise men. But they were quite surprised, since the second one was not quite as old as the first, but still, he could remember an older event.

They then honored the third one to tell his story. The third one, who was younger than the first two, said, "I remember when the fruit began to have a structure—that is, when the fruit began to be put together."*

"That story is even older," they responded.

In general, these saints were able to annul time; therefore, they had good memories. The higher a man's level, the more time is annulled for him (*Likutey Halakhoth, Milah* 4:5).

One can transcend time by closing one's eyes in pain (cf. *Likutey Moharan* 65). Then, even though he does not see, his destiny (*mazal*) sees (*Megillah* 3a). A child experiences this when it closes its eyes in pain at the time of circumcision. That is why the beggar who was above time appeared to be totally blind (*Likutey Halakhoth, Milah* 4:7).

apple from the branch. As we shall see, this is the cutting of the umbilical cord. All the allegories here are later explained by the Eagle (see *Likutey Halakhoth, Tefillin* 5:2).

an old story. From this we can understand the level of this second old man. To him, the first one's accomplishment was a joke. This is what the *Zohar* says, "each universe is like a point compared to the one above it" (*Tikkuney Zohar* 70, 123a; *Likutey Halakhoth, Tefillin* 5:1).

Thus, even though each of these elders was very high, he was like nothing compared to the one above him. This is true in every category. From each spiritual level, there is another which is infinitely higher (*Likutey Halakhoth, Yoreh Deah, Shiluach HaKen* 4:11, p. 134a).

lamp. See below.

put together. *Rakam* in Hebrew; that is, when it was "knit" or "embroidered" together. This usage is found in the verse, "I was knit together in the lowest places of the earth" (Psalms 139:15, cf. Rashi, *Metzudoth* ad loc.). In Yiddish it is, "I remember the beginning of the structure of the fruit, when the fruit began to become a fruit."

The fourth one, who was still younger, spoke up, "I also remember when the seed was brought to plant the fruit."

The fifth one, who was younger yet, said, "I also remember when the wise men invented* the seed."

The sixth one, who was younger still,* said, "I remember the taste of the fruit before it entered the fruit."

The seventh one spoke up, "I remember the fragrance of the fruit before it entered the fruit."

The eighth one said, "I remember the appearance of the fruit before it was drawn* onto the fruit."

I was also there at the time, and I was still an infant. I spoke up and said to them, "I remember all these events, and I remember *absolutely nothing*."*

"This is a very ancient story," said the wise men, "more so than all the others." They were very surprised that a child remembered more than any of them.

In the midst of this, the Great Eagle came and knocked on the tower. "Stop being poor!* Return to your treasures! Make use of your treasures!"

He then told them to leave the tower in order of their age, with the oldest going out first.

As he brought them out of the tower, he brought me, the infant, out first, since I* was actually older than all the rest, and he was bringing

---

invented. *Mamtzi* in Hebrew, which can mean invent or bring into existence. In Yiddish the word is *ois getracht*, which means "thought up."

who was younger still. Only in the Yiddish, represented by ellipses in the Hebrew.

drawn. In Yiddish it is, "I remember the appearance of the fruit before the appearance was on the fruit."

I remember absolutely nothing. *Un ich gedenk gar nisht* in Yiddish. This means that he could remember back to the time when absolutely nothing existed (*Sichoth HaRan* 149; cf. *Likutey Halakhoth, Milah* 4:5).

Stop being poor. In the world of souls, people only have a glimmer of the perception that they will have in the World to Come, which is the world that will exist after the resurrection.

I. The text uses the third person "he."

us out in order of age. Actually, the youngest was the oldest, and the oldest of them was the youngest.*

The Great Eagle then said, "I will explain the stories that each one told.

"The first one said that he remembered when they cut the apple from the branch. He was saying that he remembered* when they cut his umbilical cord.* He was saying that he remembered when he was born, and they cut his navel cord.

the oldest ... was the youngest. Thus, the blind beggar, who was the youngest, was really the oldest. Moses was both old and young. He is described as "a child weeping" (Exodus 2:6), even though he already had every perfection. Regarding him the verse states, "I was young, but I have also become old" (Psalms 37:25). Moses also attained the same perfection of vision as the blind beggar, as it is written, "his eyes were not dimmed" (Deuteronomy 34:7).

Moses was also on the level of constantly beginning anew. He thus said to God, "You have begun to show Your servant" (Deuteronomy 3:24). Even though he had received the Torah and had led the Israelites for forty years in the desert, he felt as if he had just begun.

Since Moses felt as if he had not yet begun to serve God, he was always very humble. The *Zohar* also says that with the young, Moses was young, while with the old, he was very old (*Likutey Halakhoth, Tefillin* 5:36).

remembered. The Talmud relates that Shmuel remembered the pain of his circumcision (*Yerushalmi Kethuboth* 5).

cut his umbilical cord. This was his final detachment from his mother's body. We see that this is speaking of something above the common realm, since there is no one alive who can remember having his umbilical cord cut.

This old man is alluded to in the straps of the tefillin, which must extend as far as the navel. The final stage of birth is the cutting of the umbilical cord. The Exodus from Egypt was also like the cutting of the umbilical cord. God therefore told the Israelites that before the Exodus, "Your umbilical cord was not cut" (Ezekiel 16:4). Tefillin recall the Exodus, which is the cutting of the umbilical cord, and hence, the straps must extend as far as the navel.

It is true that the other elders remembered more, but their memories are hidden in the parchments inside the tefillin boxes. The only one to whom we can relate is the first one, and he is also represented by the *retzuah*-strap which extends outside the tefillin (*Likutey Halakhoth, Tefillin* 5:16).

With the cutting of the umbilical cord, a child becomes independent of his mother. It is from the cutting of the umbilical cord that the seventy years of human life come. This is the level of stories of "ancient times." This is received from this first elder, since the others are not revealed to the external world (*Likutey Halakhoth, Tefillin* 5:20).

"The second one said that he remembered when the lamp was burning. He could also remember when he was in his mother's womb, with a lamp burning over his head.*

"The third one said that he remembered when the fruit began to form. He could remember when his body began to knit together as the fetus took its form.

"The fourth one said that he remembered when the seed was brought to be planted. He remembered how the drop was emitted at the time of conception.*

On a deeper Kabbalistic level, there are four levels in the human body: bone, sinews, flesh, and skin. Skin is therefore an aspect of Malkhuth, the lowest of the four levels. The cutting of the navel cord thus represents the rectification of the skin, the outermost level of the body. The bones, sinews, and flesh are rectified within the body, but the skin is not rectified until the umbilical cord is cut.

The *partzufim* (Divine personae) stand in such a way that each one ends at the level of the navel of the one above it. Hence, when the first elder remembers his navel cord, he is actually speaking of the link between the supernal *partzufim* and universes. This process begins when the world of *nekudim* (dots) comes out under the navel of Adam Kadmon (*Likutey Halakhoth, Tefillin* 5:34).

This is also related to the concept of the Holy Land. Jerusalem is thus called "the navel of the earth" (*Zimrath HaAretz*).

lamp burning over his head. The Talmud teaches that before a child is born, while it is in the womb, it has a lamp over its head with which it looks from one end of the universe to the other (*Niddah* 30b). This is based on Job's words, "Oh, that I was as in the months of old, in the days when God watched over me, when *His lamp shone above my head*, and I walked through darkness by His light" (Job 29:2,3). The light with which one can see from one end of the earth to the other is the light that God created at the very beginning, and then put aside for the righteous in the World to Come. The Midrash states explicitly that with this light one can see from one end of the universe to the other (Rashi on Genesis 1:4; *Likutey Halakhoth, Tefillin* 5:1). An unborn child can have such perception, since evil has no grasp on a child before he is born (*Anaf Yosef*, on *Eyn Yaakov, Niddah* 30b).

Death can be seen as a birth into a new dimension. Therefore, it is customary to light a lamp for the death anniversary (*yahrzeit*) of a close relative. The *yahrzeit* lamp parallels the lamp that burns over a child's head before he is born (*Likutey Halakhoth, Tefillin* 5:43).

of conception. It is significant to note that among these eight elders, the first four remember events that occurred in the womb, while the last four remember events that preceded the womb. Thus, in a sense, the first four have a feminine memory, while the second four have a male memory (that pertains to their fathers).

"The fifth one remembered the wise men who discovered the seed. He remembered when the seed was still in the brain.* The brain's mental power gives rise to the drop.

"The sixth one remembered the taste. This is the *nefesh*–soul.*

This is related to the eight readings in the tefillin, of which four are in the head tefillin and four are in the hand tefillin. The hand tefillin is a female aspect, so its four readings pertain to the first four elders. The head tefillin, on the other hand, represents the male aspect, and hence, the second four elders (*Likutey Halakhoth, Tefillin* 5:3). The significance of this is discussed somewhat.

The four readings in the tefillin are Sh'ma (Deuteronomy 6:4–9), *Vahaya im shamoa* (Deuteronomy 11:13–21), *Kadesh* (Exodus 13:2–10), and *Vahaya ki yaviakha* (Exodus 13:11–16). Respectively, they speak of faith in God, keeping the commandments, sanctification of the firstborn, and entering the promised land.

The Sh'ma, which speaks of our relationship to God, parallels the first elder, who remembers conception and intercourse. Sh'ma speaks of unity, and in a sense, this unity is like a joining of Israel and God. Indeed, the *Zohar* states that the seven blessings surrounding the Sh'ma (three in the morning and four in the evening) are the *Sheva Berakhoth* (seven marital blessings) for this union.

Vahaya im shamoa, which speaks of our obligation to keep the commandments, parallels the second elder, who remembered when his body began to form. There are 613 commandments, 248 positive, and 365 negative, paralleling the 248 limbs and 365 nerves in the body. Hence, the perfection of the body's formation is the keeping of the commandments.

Kadesh, the third reading, parallels the one who remembered the light over his head. *Kadesh* speaks of the miracles surrounding the Exodus, when God's glory was revealed to the Israelites. This revelation parallels the light over the child's head. The ten plagues, of which the killing of the firstborn was the last, marked the end of the "pregnancy" of the Israelites. The "lamp over their head" may also allude to the giving of the Torah, which was the end of the "pregnancy" of the Jewish people.

VaHaya ki yaviakha relates to entering the Holy Land. This is the cutting of the umbilical cord of the Israelites. As long as they were in the desert, they were nourished by the manna, food which came directly from God, very much as a child is nourished through its navel cord. But when they entered the Holy Land, the manna stopped, and they had to provide their own food. This parallels the cutting of the navel cord in a child (cf. *Likutey Halakhoth, Tefillin* 5:12, 5:15).

seed was still in the brain. It is a Kabbalistic teaching that the sperm has its origin in the father's brain. This might mean that the main thing that the father imparts in the sperm is information, on the level of Chokhmah. In any case, we see that the fifth elder has a memory that transcends the womb and goes back to his father.

nefesh–soul. The Torah uses three words for the soul: *nefesh* (meaning rest), *ruach* (meaning "wind"), and *neshamah* (meaning "breath"). The Kabbalists liken it to a glassblower,

"The seventh one remembered the fragrance. This is the *ruach*–spirit.*

"The eighth one remembered the appearance. This is the *neshamah*–essence.*

"Finally, there was the child who said that he remembered absolutely nothing. He is higher than all the rest, since he remembered

where the process begins with his breath, extends through his blowing tube as wind, and then comes to rest in the vessel being formed.

When this elder said that he remembers when the taste was placed in the fruit, he was indicating that he remembered when his *nefesh*–soul was drawn from on high (*Likutey Halakhoth, Tefillin; Likutey Halakhoth, Tefillath Minchah* 7:93).

Taste requires actual contact with the thing being tasted. In a similar manner, the *nefesh*–soul is in direct contact with the body.

The three parts of the soul, *nefesh, ruach,* and *neshamah,* represent the three inner lights of the person, enclosed within the form of his body. Similarly, the body has three inner parts, bone, sinew, and flesh, enclosed within the skin. The first elders recalled the beginnings of bone, sinew, flesh, and skin, while the second group recalled the *nefesh, ruach, neshamah,* and form (*Likutey Halakhoth, Tefillin* 5:34).

ruach–spirit. *Ruach* means "wind," and fragrance is carried by the wind.

Furthermore, taste involves the mouth, which represents the sefirah of Malkhuth and parallels the *nefesh.* Smell involves the nose, which represents Zer Anpin and parallels the *ruach.*

neshamah–essence. Thus, there are eight elders, four with a feminine memory (involving their relationships with their mothers), and four with a masculine memory (involving their existence before conception).

As mentioned earlier, these represent the eight readings in the tefillin. The four in the head tefillin represent the four elders with masculine memories, while the four in the hand tefillin represent the four with feminine memories (*Likutey Halakhoth, Tefillin* 5:3).

The eight elders also parallel the eight "rectifications" (*tikkunim*) of Aaron's beard. These parallel the eight priestly vestments. The blind beggar, the ninth one, then represents Moses. It is thus written, "The midwives feared God, and He made for them houses" (Exodus 1:21). Our sages say that one of these midwives was Yocheved, and the "houses" speak of Moses and Aaron. It is also taught that the "houses" represent the tefillin, since the boxes are called *batim,* which literally means "houses." Thus, Moses and Aaron in a sense represent the tefillin, as well as the nine elders here (*Likutey Halakhoth, Tefillin* 5:36).

It is also taught that in the Makhpelah Cave, four pairs were buried: Adam and Eve, Abraham and Sarah, Isaac and Rebecca, and Jacob and Leah (*Eruvin* 53a). These eight individuals also parallel the eight portions in the tefillin, and hence, the eight elders. Thus, again, four of the elders have masculine memories, and four have feminine memories (*Likutey Halakhoth, Tefillin* 5:39).

even what was before the *nefesh*–soul, the *ruach*–spirit, and the *neshamah*–essence. This is the concept of Nothingness."*

The eight elders can also be seen as paralleling the eight days preceding circumcision. The Kabbalistic texts teach that cutting off the foreskin (*chitukh*) annuls the three Klipoth, while the uncovering of the glans (*periyah*) annuls the *klipath nogah*, which is a mixture of good and bad. The *chitukh* is represented by the eight elders, while the *periyah* is represented by the blind beggar, who is higher than all of them (*Likutey Halakhoth, Milah* 4:5, 4:9; cf. *Likutey Moharan* 72).

Nothingness. This is the level which no thought can grasp. Therefore it is experienced as Nothingness.

If the eight elders represent the eight readings in the tefillin, the blind beggar would represent the source of their holiness. He is so high that his concept cannot be included in any of the readings. He is on a level that touches the Infinite (*Ain Sof*). He cannot remember anything because his mind is above the concept of memory. He remembers everything that the other elders do, but in his case, this cannot be called memory at all. He is the root of memory, much higher than memory (*Likutey Halakhoth, Tefillin* 5:3; see *Chokhmah U'Tevunah* 16).

This beggar was blind, because he had rectified his eyes completely. Since the tefillin are worn "between the eyes," this is the source of the light of the eight readings in the tefillin. From there it extends to the strap that comes down to the navel, which represents the first elder, who gives the light to the world (*Likutey Halakhoth, Tefillin* 5:34).

In Kabbalah, it is taught that the light from the eyes of Adam Kadmon is revealed as the world of *nekudim* (dots) below his navel (*Etz Chaim, Shaar HaNekudim*). This light of *nekudim* is taken from his eyes, and then channeled through the eight "rectifications" of his beard. The breaking of vessels comes from his eyes, and it is for this reason that in warning us to keep from sin, the Torah says, "Do not stray after your eyes" (Numbers 15:39). The blind beggar purifies his eyes and rectifies both this concept and the breaking of vessels (ibid.).

Marriage is a very high concept. The union of man and woman can bring down a soul from the highest reaches. This is why the first beggar came and told them about memories of birth, and even before conception. He is telling them the levels they will have to reach to bring down a soul to the world. The blind beggar himself then tells them that they must even reach up to the level of Nothingness to bring down a soul (*Likutey Halakhoth, Tefillath Minchah* 7:93).

In one way, the blind beggar doesn't remember anything because he remembers what the soul was like even before the *tzimtzum*. Since the Messiah comes from the highest level, he can rectify even the lowest (ibid.).

When a person is sexually pure, he is connected to the source of souls. This is the concept of circumcision, which relates to the elders, as mentioned earlier. When a person commits sexual misdeeds, the penalty is *KaReT*, being cut off before one's time, which is the opposite of old age. The old men in the story were on a level of *KeTeR*, which has the same letters as *kareth*, but is its rectification. *Kether* is related to Arikh Anpin,

He then said to them, "Return to your ships, which are your bodies.* They were shattered, but they will be rebuilt. Now go back to them." With that, he blessed them.

The Great Eagle then said to me, "You come with me, since you are just like me. You are very old, and at the same time very young; you have not yet begun to live, but you are extremely old. I am the same, since I am old and at the same time, I am young ..."

Therefore, I have the word of the Great Eagle that I have lived a very long life.

Now, I am giving you my long life as a wedding present.*

When the beggar said this, there was tremendous joy and rejoicing there.*

The Second Day*

On the second of the seven days of celebration,* the couple began to

whose beard has thirteen rectifications. These parallel the thirteen covenants that were made with regard to circumcision (*Nedarim* 31b).

Thus, a true tzaddik, who is sexually pure and keeps the covenant of Abraham, is considered old. He gets his power from the blind beggar who is the highest of these old men (*Likutey Halakhoth, Milah* 4:8).

The Talmud teaches that the commandment, "Do not stray after your eyes" is a commandment specifically related to sexual chastity. The blind beggar perfected this to its highest degree, and therefore also attained the highest level of sexual chastity. Thus, he could see into the highest reaches from where the soul was drawn.

which are your bodies. Here we see explicitly that the ships represent the body. This is speaking of the resurrection of the dead (*Rimzey Maasioth*).

wedding present. *Drasha geshank*, see above. The beggars gave these gifts at the wedding, because a wedding is the first stage of the coupling of man and woman that brings souls down to the world. To bring down a soul requires all the powers of the seven sefiroth (*Likutey Halakhoth, Tefillath Minchah* 7:93).

there. At this point, Rabbi Nachman's attendant, Reb Michel (*Yemey Moharnat*, p. 21b), came in and told Rabbi Nathan to leave, since it was time for the Rebbe's meal (*Sichoth HaRan* 149).

The Second Day. On Wednesday, April 4, after Rabbi Nachman had eaten and taken a short nap, Rabbi Nathan returned, telling the Rebbe how the wealthy people in Berdichev are constantly in debt. He quoted the verse, "God has set the world in their heart, so that men cannot find out God's deeds from the beginning to the end" (Ecclesiastes 3:11). Rabbi Nachman said, "Is this not our tale? Where are we holding now?" He then began

remember the second beggar, the deaf one, who had sustained them and given them bread. They wept and yearned, "How can we bring here the deaf beggar who sustained us?"

While they were yearning for him, he suddenly appeared and said, "Here I am!" He fell on them and kissed them.

He then said to them: Now I will give you a gift that you should be like me. You should live a good life* like mine. I originally gave you this as a blessing, but now, as your wedding present, I am giving you this as an unrestricted gift.

You think that I am deaf. I am not deaf at all. But the whole world does not amount to anything to me that I should listen* to its shortcomings.

All sounds come from deficiencies,* since everyone cries out

to tell the story of the second day (*Sichoth HaRan* 149; *Likutey Halakhoth, Evven HaEzer, P'ru U'R'vu* 3:32).

seven days of celebration. It is customary to make a feast for the first seven days after a wedding, during which the seven nuptial blessings (*Sheva Berakhoth*) are recited. We find this at the weddings of Jacob (Genesis 29:27) and Samson (Judges 14:12). The seven days of celebration parallel the seven days of creation.

good life. This is a life that reflects the life in the World to Come, living on a high spiritual plane. The Israelites were worthy of a good life in the Land of Israel, since it was a "land that has no lack" (Deuteronomy 8:9; *Zimrath HaAretz*).

that I should listen. The deaf beggar did not want to derive any enjoyment from hearing the sounds of the world (*Likutey Halakhoth, Choshen Mishpat, HaOseh Sheliach LiG'both Chovo* 2:10, p. 82a).

deficiencies. *Chasronoth.* All worldly sounds are an echo of the True Voice (*Likutey Moharan Tinyana* 23). This echo is the source of all the deficiencies in the world. It is the sound of worldly foolishness that results from the constriction (*tzimtzum*).

The Torah is the direct sound that was the power of all creation. An echo is a direct sound that strikes a barrier and is reflected. In the original *tzimtzum*, there was a thin line of Light that entered the Vacated Space. This was the light of the Torah. It struck the central point and produced the reflected light, or the echo.

The ring of Light was the direct voice with which all things were created, as it is written, "With God's Word the heavens were made" (Psalms 33:6). When this voice hits the central point, which is the final barrier of the *tzimtzum*, it creates an echo. This is so much like the direct Voice, that one can be mistaken and think it to be the True Voice. This is the source of Free Will (*Likutey Halakhoth, Evven HaEzer, P'ru U'R'vu* 3:32).

The Echo is lacking in Divine Power and good. Since this echo is the source of all worldly sounds, they are not holy; they have some worldly desire in them (ibid. 3:34).

because of what he is lacking. Even all the joys of the world are the result of lacks, since it is only because one has a lack that one rejoices when this lack is filled. But the entire world does not amount to anything for me that I should allow its deficiencies to enter my ears.*

I have a good life where nothing is lacking. I have the word* of the Land of Wealth* that I live the good life. (His good life was that he had bread to eat* and water to drink.)

He then told them the story:

There was a land that had lots of wealth and great treasures.* Once, the people got together, and each one began to boast about how he lived the good life. Each one related exactly what kind of good life he had.

I spoke up and said, "I am living a good life that is better than your good life. If you want proof, let me tell you about a certain land. If you are truly living a good life, let's see if you can save this land.*

"This land had a garden.* This garden had fruit which had every taste in the world. It also had every fragrance in the world. It also had

to enter my ears. A true tzaddik lacks nothing, and therefore does not have any need to hear any worldly sounds. He therefore appears to be deaf (*Likutey Etzoth* B, *Tzaddik* 99).

word. *Haskamah*, see above p. 13.

Land of Wealth. The wealthy people in this land were the great tzaddikim, who were wealthy in good deeds (*Rimzey Maasioth*). This is in contrast to the Land of Wealth in the story of "The Master of Prayer" (in *The Lost Princess*).

bread to eat... A true tzaddik can find all tastes in bread and water (*Rimzey Maasioth*). It is also taught, "This is the way of Torah, eat bread and salt, and drink water by measure" (*Avoth* 6:4). The Mishnah concludes, "If you do this, happy are you, and it shall be good for you—happy are you in this world, and it shall be good for you in the World to Come."

The deaf beggar is to be compared in this respect to the Simpleton in "The Sophisticate and the Simpleton" (in *The Lost Princess*) who also tasted all foods in his bread.

great treasures. Tzaddikim have great spiritual treasures (*Rimzey Maasioth*). These are the treasures of good life that they have stored in the World to Come (*Likutey Etzoth* B, *Tzaddik* 90). King Monvoz thus said, "My ancestors amassed treasures in this world, but I will amass treasures in the World to Come" (*Bava Bathra* 11a).

save this land. There are levels that can only be helped by the greatest possible tzaddik (*Likutey Etzoth* B, *Tzaddik* 90).

garden. The world of the spiritual.

every sight in the world—every color and every kind of flower.*
Everything was in that garden.

"There was a gardener* in charge of this garden. Because of that
garden, the people of that land lived a good life.*

"The gardener then vanished.* With no one tending the garden,
everything in the garden naturally withered and died. Nevertheless, the
people were still able to live from the wild plants* that grew in the garden.

"A cruel king* then attacked the land, but he was not able to do
anything to the people. He therefore decided to ruin the good life that
the land had from the garden. However, he did not ruin the garden
itself. Instead, he left three groups of servants.*

"He ordered them to follow his instructions, and thus ruin the people's sense of taste. As a result of what they did, whenever anyone
tasted anything, it had the taste of a rotten carcass.*

"They also ruined the sense of smell. Every fragrance that the people smelled had the stench of galbanum.*

"They also destroyed the sense of sight. They dimmed the people's

---

flower. *Kviyatin* in Yiddish.

gardener. *Gradnik* in Yiddish. The *Zohar* states that the gardener is the tzaddik who tends
the spiritual world and distributes its power (*Zohar* 2:166b; *Likutey Moharan* 65; *Rimzey
Maasioth*; cf. *Kedushath Shabbath*; *Sichoth HaRan* 252).

lived a good life. Everyone in the world can have a good life from the spiritual world
(*Likutey Etzoth* B, *Tzaddik* 90).

vanished. The gardener vanished because of our sins (ibid.).

wild plants. The spiritual realm has enough to nourish the world even without the tzaddik
(cf. ibid.).

cruel king. The Evil One (*Likutey Etzoth* B, *Tzaddik* 90).

three groups of servants. They were to ruin the taste, sight, and fragrance. In a sense,
they were to ruin the concept of the Sabbath. The preparations for the Sabbath include
setting the table (taste), lighting a lamp (sight), and making the bed (fragrance, see
below) (*Kedushath Shabbath*).

rotten carcass. *Nevelah.*

galbanum. *Chelbanah* in Hebrew. This was one of the ingredients of the Temple incense
(Exodus 30:34).

eyes, as if they were covered with clouds and mists.*

"All this was done at the cruel king's command. Now if you are truly living the good life, let's see if you can save them. I am telling you this because, if you do not save them, then the damage that has stricken this land can also harm you.'*

The wealthy people set off toward that land, and I also went with them. While travelling, each of them lived the good life in his way, since each one had taken along his treasures.

However, as soon as they came near that land, their sense of taste began to go bad. They also began to feel that other things were also being spoiled for them.

I said to them, "You have not even entered the land yet, and your sense of taste etc. is ruined... What will happen once you actually get there? How will you be able to save them?"

I then took my bread and water and gave some to them. As soon as they tasted* my bread and water, their sense of taste was remedied.* The same was true of their sense of smell and the like...

Meanwhile, the people of the land that had the garden began to look for ways to remedy their senses that had been ruined.... Their conclusion involved the Land of Wealth from which I was now coming. It seemed that their lost gardener who had provided them with the good life had the same roots as the people of the Land of Wealth, who also had a good life. Therefore, their plan was to send a delegation to the Land of Wealth, who would certainly be able to help them.

They sent messengers to the Land of Wealth. Along the way, the messengers met the people from the Land of Wealth, with whom I had gone.

clouds and mists. These are the clouds that cover the eye (*Likutey Etzoth* B, *Tzaddik* 90).

can also harm you. The Talmud thus teaches that an incomplete tzaddik can be "swallowed" by evil. Only a complete tzaddik is not touched by it (*Berakhoth* 7b; Rabbi Rosenfeld).

tasted. "Taste and see that God is good..." (Psalms 34:9).

remedied. When people want to remedy things, they go to the great tzaddikim. But in the end, even these tzaddikim need the power of the greatest tzaddik, who here is represented by the deaf beggar (*Likutey Etzoth* B, *Tzaddik* 91).

The true tzaddik shares his good life with others, and he can then undo any spiritual damage that they may have experienced.

"Where are you going?" they asked the messengers.

"We are going to the Land of Wealth," they replied. "We want them to help us."

"We ourselves are from the Land of Wealth," said the others. "We are on our way to you."

I said to the others, "Actually, you need me. You cannot go there yourselves,* as you have already seen. You stay here. I will go with the messengers, and help the land."

I went with them, and we came to a city in the land. When I arrived, I saw a few people come and begin to tell jokes.* Then other people gathered around, and they told jokes, giggling and laughing.

When I listened more carefully,* I realized that they were telling obscene jokes.* One made an obscene remark, and another would repeat it in a more subtle fashion. Some would laugh, another would enjoy it.

I then went to another city, and saw two people arguing about a business deal. They went to court to settle the affair, and the court ruled that one was liable and the other innocent. However, as soon as they left the court, they once again began to argue. They said that they did not like the decision of this court, and wanted another court. Since both of them wanted to try the case in another court, they chose another one. But after the case was tried, one of the people began arguing with someone else, and these two chose another court.* The place was thus full of strife and argument. The people needed so many courts that the entire city was full of courts.

You cannot go there yourselves. In order to rectify the world, all tzaddikim need the help of the greatest tzaddik. There are places where other tzaddikim cannot go to rectify things (*Chayay Nefesh* 34; see *Likutey Moharan* 64).

jokes. *Halatzah* in Hebrew; *vertil* in Yiddish.

listened more carefully. Literally, "inclined my ear."

obscene jokes. *Nivul peh*, which means "profanity." The word *nivul* shares the same root as *nevelah*, which denotes a rotten carcass. Since they spoke *nivul*, all food tasted like *nevelah*, as we shall see.

chose another court. Rabbi Nachman is referring to a system such as exists in Jewish jurisprudence, where in addition to standing courts, people can set up ad hoc courts to judge their cases. Each party in litigation chooses one judge, and then the two judges decide on a third, thus making a three-judge ad hoc court.

I observed all this, and realized that there was no truth there. Today a judge might decide in one person's favor and show him special consideration, and tomorrow the other would return the favor. Everything was based on bribery, with no sense of the truth.*

I also noticed that the people were totally immoral sexually. Sexual immorality was so prevalent, that everything seemed permissible* to them.

I said to them, "This is the reason that the taste, the fragrance, and the appearance have been spoiled for you. This cruel king left with you three groups of his servants, and they ruined the land.

"These servants began by speaking in a profane manner among themselves, and this brought profanity to the land. As a result of the profanity,* the sense of taste became ruined, and everything tastes like a rotten carcass.

"They also brought bribery into the land. As a result, the eyes were dimmed, and the sense of sight was ruined, since 'Bribery blinds the eyes of the wise' (Deuteronomy 16:19).

"Also, they brought sexual immorality into the land. This caused the sense of smell to be ruined.*

"Therefore, you must correct these three wrongs in your land. Find

no sense of the truth. From here we see how important a true system of justice is (*Rimzey Maasioth*).

everything seemed permissible. Literally, "became like permissible." This is based on the Talmudic teaching, "When a person sins, and repeats the act, it becomes to him as if it were permissible" (*Yoma* 86b).

as a result of the profanity. See above p. 27. The first step in the downfall of the people was listening to profanity. Since the deaf beggar could not "hear" it, he was not affected. The story says that he heard it, but he did not hear any of the worldly evil in it.

The perfection of the Hebrew language is the rectification for the profanity. It is thus taught that there are no profane words in Hebrew, and for this reason it is called "the Holy Tongue" (*Kedushath Shabbath*).

smell ... ruined. This teaches that one must be very careful regarding sexual immorality, since it destroys one's sense of smell (*Rimzey Maasioth*).

It is thus taught that the prophet Elisha had a bed that had the fragrance of the Garden of Eden because he always kept himself sexually pure (*Zohar* 2:44a; *Kedushath Shabbath*). The Talmud also teaches that the young men of Israel have a beautiful fragrance when they are sexually pure (*Berakhoth* 43b; *Parparoth LeChokhmah* ad loc.).

out who the king's servants are, and drive them away.* When you correct these three wrongs, then not only will you restore the taste, fragrance and appearance, but the missing gardener will also be able to be found."

The people did this, and began to rid the land of these three wrongs. They investigated the king's agents and when they captured them, they asked, "Where do you come from?" When they determined that they were the cruel king's agents, they banished them. The land was thus rectified of the three wrongs.

While this was going on, there was sudden excitement. People began to say, "There is a crazy man who is going around, saying that he is the gardener.* Everyone thought that he was crazy, so they threw stones at him and drove him away. But somehow, it is possible that he is the one! Maybe he is actually the gardener!"

The men who were trying to remedy the land went and brought him before them. I said, "Certainly this is really the gardener!"

Therefore, I have the word of the Land of Wealth that I live the good life, since I was able to rectify this land.*

Now my gift to you is my good life.

When he finished speaking, there was great joy and tremendous rejoicing.

Similarly, all the beggars were to return and come to the wedding, giving the couple wedding presents that they should be like them. What they had originally given as a blessing, they gave as a wedding present. The first one thus gave them a gift of long life, while the second one gave them a gift of a good life.

---

drive them away. The good life involves spiritual sight, taste, and fragrance. In order to be worthy of it, one must keep away from people who are involved in the sins that destroy these spiritual senses (*Rimzey Maasioth*).

saying that he is the gardener. When someone claims to be the true tzaddik, people laugh and throw stones at him (*Likutey Etzoth* B, *Tzaddik* 90). People who have lost their senses of taste, smell, and sight cannot recognize the true gardener.

rectify this land. The reason that he could rectify the land was because he himself did not lack anything. Therefore, nothing of the land could affect him (*Rimzey Maasioth*).

The Third Day*

On the third day, the couple once again began to reminisce, and they wept and yearned, "How can we bring the third beggar who had a speech defect?" All of a sudden he appeared and said, "Here I am!" He fell on them and kissed them.

He then said: At first I blessed you that you should be like me. Now I am giving you as a wedding present that you should be like me.

You think that I have a speech defect. I do not have a speech defect at all. Rather, all the words in the world which do not praise God do not have any perfection* in them. I therefore seem to have a speech defect, since I cannot speak words which lack perfection. But actually, I do not have a speech defect at all. Quite the contrary, I am a wonderful orator* and speaker. I can speak in parables* and lyric* that are so wonderful that there is no created thing* in the world that does not want to hear me.

The parables and lyrics that I know contain all wisdom.* Regarding this, I have the word* of a great man, who is called the True

The Third Day. The stories of the third and fourth days were told on the subsequent Friday night (April 6) (*Sichoth HaRan* 149). At that time, Rabbi Nachman's grandson was very sick (*Yemey Moharnat* 32b). Rabbi Nachman discussed how the heart is pursued. He then asked, "Where are we holding?" Then he began the story of the third day (*Sichoth HaRan* 151).

The 61st psalm pertains to the story of the third day, as we shall see (end of story). Rabbi Nachman told this part of the story with great longing, tremendous reverence, and a wonderful attachment to God. From this, everyone present could understand that this part of the story contained many wondrous concepts (*Rimzey Maasioth*).

do not have any perfection. This teaches the importance of being careful about what one says. The mute beggar felt that any words that did not praise God were imperfect, and he could not pronounce them (*Rimzey Maasioth*). This was also a manifestation of his not wanting to have anything to do with the worldly (*Likutey Halakhoth, Choshen Mishpat, HaOseh Sheliach LiG'both Chovo* 2:10, p. 82a).

wonderful orator. Like Moses, who was a stutterer, but said the greatest things in the world. Since God created the world with speech, this power is among the greatest in the world.

parables. *Chidoth.*

lyric. In Hebrew it is "*shirim* which are *luder*," but in Yiddish it is "*shirim* and *luder*."

created thing. Including even the highest spiritual beings (*Rimzey Maasioth*).

all wisdom. Since all creation was accomplished through words, words contain all wisdom. One who has perfected the power of speech thus has access to all wisdom.

word. *Haskamah.* See above p. 13.

Man of Kindness.* There is an entire story about this.

Once all the wise men were sitting together, and each one boasted of his wisdom.

One boasted that with his wisdom he had discovered how to make iron.

One boasted that he had discovered another type of metal.

One boasted that with his wisdom he had discovered how to make silver, which is more valuable.

One boasted that he had discovered how to make gold.

One boasted that he had discovered how to make weapons.

One boasted that he had invented ways of making metals from ingredients out of which metals are not usually made.

One boasted about other sciences, since with these sciences such things as saltpeter* and gunpowder* were invented.

Thus, each one boasted about his wisdom.

Finally, one of them spoke up and said, "I am wiser than all of you; I am wise like the day."

The others did not understand what he meant when he said that he was wise like the day.

He explained to them, "If all your wisdom was put together, it would only amount to a single hour. It is true that each science is derived from a particular day, depending on what was created on that day. Nevertheless, all the sciences merely involve combining* things in different ways. Therefore, each science is only derived from combinations of things created on that day. With true wisdom, one can gather all these sciences into a single hour. But I am wise like a full day."

This was the boast of the last wise man.

I spoke up and said to him, "Like which day?"*

True Man of Kindness. In Yiddish, *"der groiser man, der emes-er ish chesed."* This is the exact wording of our Rabbi of blessed memory.

saltpeter. *Salitra.*

gunpowder. *Pilver.*

combining. Literally, "combinations," *harkvoth* in Hebrew.

Like Which Day. The text adds, "That is, like which day are you wise?"

Speaking of me, this wise man replied, "This man is even wiser than I am, since he can ask, 'Like which day?' However, I am wise like any day you prefer."

Now you might ask why a person who can ask, "Like which day?" is wiser than one who is as wise as any day he desires. This, however, involves a story. It concerns the True Man of Kindness,* who is actually a very great man.

I go around and gather all true kindness and bring it to the True Man of Kindness. Time itself is something that was created, and time exists primarily* as a result of true kindness. I therefore go around gathering all true kindness, and bring it to the True Man of Kindness.

There is a mountain. On the mountain there is a stone. From this stone, flows a Spring.*

Everything has a heart.* Therefore the world as a whole also has a heart.* The Heart of the World has a complete body,* with face,

---

True Man of Kindness. This is alluded to in the key psalm, "May he be enthroned before God forever, appoint mercy and truth so that they will preserve him" (Psalms 61:8).

The main trait of this man was kindness, Chesed in Hebrew. It is taught that charity is not perfect except when it is given with kindness, as it is written, "Sow charity for yourselves, and reap according to Chesed" (Hosea 10:12; *Sukkah* 49b; *Likutey Halakhoth, Melamdim* 4:13).

time exists primarily ... Time comes into existence primarily through charity and kindness (*Likutey Halakhoth, Melamdim* 4:13). This teaching is based on the verse, "To tell Your Chesed in the morning, and Your faith by night" (Psalms 92:3; *Zimrath HaAretz*). In order to have a share in this process, one must do charity and kind deeds (*Likutey Etzoth B, Tzedakah* 8).

Kabbalistically, time comes into existence as a result of the actions of the lower sefiroth (*Pardes Rimonim*). These sefiroth begin with Chesed, and hence, Chesed is the source of time.

Spring. This Spring is the point which is the source of the rectification of all worlds. It is the source of all good points that a person can find in himself (*Likutey Halakhoth, Melamdim* 4:13; see *Likutey Moharan* 282). This point is Chokhmah (*Likutey Moharan* 34:5). Hence, the Spring in the story is Chokhmah (*Zohar* 2:42b). In this sense, the Spring can also be seen as the brain (*Kedushath Shabbath*).

heart. Kabbalistically, the heart always represents Binah. Hence, the relationship between the heart and the Spring is basically the relationship between Chokhmah and Binah.

also has a heart. This heart is the root of all Jewish hearts (*Rimzey Maasioth*). In another sense, the Temple was the heart of the world (*Zimrath HaAretz*).

hands, and feet... However, a toenail of the Heart of the World has more of the essential nature of a heart* than the heart of anything else.

The mountain with the stone and the spring stands at one end of the world. The Heart of the World stands at the opposite end of the world. The Heart of the World faces the Spring and constantly longs and yearns* to come to the Spring. It has a very, very great longing, and it cries out* very much that it should be able to come to the Spring.

The Spring also yearns for the Heart.

The Heart has two things* that make it weak.

First, the sun* pursues it* and burns it.* This is because it has

complete body. The sefirah of Binah becomes the *partzuf* of *imma* (mother), which is a spiritual entity having the form of a human body.

essential nature of a heart. More concisely, "hearty," *meluvav* in Hebrew; *hartziker* in Yiddish.

longs and yearns. The existence of the universal Heart does not depend on its getting to the Spring, but only on its yearning for the Spring.

cries out. King David identified with the Heart of the World, and in the key psalm, he cried out, "From the ends of the earth I call to You. When my heart is faint, lead me to a rock that is too high for me" (Psalms 61:3). Rabbi Nachman states this allusion explicitly (end of story).

From the yearning and crying out of this Heart comes the yearning and crying out in all prayer and in all *hithbodeduth*–meditation (*Likutey Halakhoth, Melamdim* 4:13).

two things. The two things that make it weak are the sun, and its yearning for the Spring. The sun represents worldly desire, while the Spring represents spiritual desire. But worldly desire and unfulfilled spiritual desire weaken the Heart (*Likutey Halakhoth, Melamdim* 4:13).

sun. All worldly desires are considered "under the sun," as it is written, "What profit does a man have of all his labor which he does under the sun" (Ecclesiastes 1:3). All evil is "under the sun," that is under the realm of time. Above time, there is no evil. But time is related to the sun, for time is counted by the solar day. Although the Heart is pure and holy, it is sick because of what is done "under the sun" (*Likutey Halakhoth, Melamdim* 4:13).

pursues it. This part of the story began with Rabbi Nachman discussing "the Heart that is pursued" (*Sichoth HaRan* 151).

burns it. This is the "heat" of the Evil Urge, the concept of fallen love. The Heart's love is directed toward the Spring, but the "sun" wants to annul this love and make it involved in worldly love and lust. The Evil Urge thus pursues the heart of the Jew and tries to burn it (*Likutey Halakhoth, Melamdim* 4:13).

such a desire, yearning to go and be close to the Spring.

The second thing that weakens the Heart is the great longing and yearning that it constantly has toward the Spring. It longs and yearns so much that its soul goes out, and it cries out. It constantly stands facing the Spring, and cries out, "Help!"* desiring it so very much.

When the Heart wants to rest a bit and catch its breath, a great bird* comes and spreads its wings over it, protecting it* from the sun. It then can relax a bit. However, even when it is resting, it looks toward the Spring and yearns for it.

One may wonder, since it yearns for it so much, why does it not go to the Spring?

However, if it were to come close to the mountain, then it would no longer see the peak.* It then could not gaze at the Spring, and if it stopped looking at the Spring, it would die, since its main source of life is the Spring. When it stands facing the mountain, it can see the peak upon which the Spring is, but as soon as it comes close to the mountain, the peak is hidden from its eyes. This is clearly demonstrable. If it could not see the Spring, then it would die.*

Help. *Na Gevalt.*

great bird. The wings of this bird are alluded to in the key psalm, "I will take refuge in the cover of Your wings" (Psalms 61:5) (end of story).

The wings protecting the Heart are very much like the wings of the cherubim that protected the holy ark (Exodus 25:20; *Zimrath HaAretz*). The bird's wings also represent the lungs, which protect the Heart and nourish it (*Likutey Halakhoth, Melamdim* 4:17; *Kedushath Shabbath*).

protecting it. The bird's wings represent the lungs. It is taught that, if not for the wings of the lungs that blow on the heart, the heat of the heart would burn the entire body (*Tikkuney Zohar* 13, 27b). Rabbi Nachman teaches that the power of speech involving prayer and Torah study cools down the desires of the heart and allows a person to survive (*Likutey Moharan* 78). The heart may burn for worldly things, but the power of the "wings" of prayer and Torah study protect it from consuming the body.

The bird also protects the Heart from weakness due to its yearning for the Spring. If a person does not have too much worldly desire, he is not weakened by his spiritual desire. Because of the bird, the Heart can look at the Spring with proper measure, so that it is not weakened by it (*Likutey Halakhoth, Melamdim* 4:13).

peak. *Shpitz* in Yiddish. *Shipua* in Hebrew, which has the connotation of inclination.

would die. Expressed idiomatically, "Its soul would leave it."

If the Heart died, then the entire world would cease to exist. The Heart is the life-force of all things, and nothing can exist without a heart.

It is for this reason that it cannot go to the Spring. It therefore stands facing it, yearning and crying out.*

Time does not exist for the Spring. The Spring is not inside of time* at all. The Spring only has time because the Heart gives it as a gift for one day.

However, when the time comes for the day to come to a close, then at the end of the day, the Spring will not have any more time, and it will therefore die. This in turn would cause the Heart to die. The entire world would then cease to exist.*

Toward the end of the day,* they begin to take leave* of each other. At that time, they begin to speak to one another in wonderful parables and lyrics* with great love and tremendous desire.

---

yearning and crying out. When the Heart gazes at the Spring, the breaking of vessels is rectified, and as a result, everything else is also rectified (*Likutey Halakhoth, Melamdim* 4:13). In general, this teaches that the world exists primarily because of the longing and desire for the holy on the part of people's hearts. Although the Heart cannot approach the Spring, its longing is enough for it to accomplish this purpose (*Likutey Etzoth* B, *Ratzon* 5).

not inside of time. The Yiddish adds, "That is, the Spring does not have any time whatsoever. That is, it has no day, and no time in the world. This is because it is very much higher than the time of the world."

The Spring is very much like God, who is the Creator of time, and is hence above time (cf. *Likutey Halakhoth, Tzitzith* 3:15). It is significant to note that the third beggar was able to transcend time, while the fifth one was able to transcend space.

cease to exist. This is prevented by the True Man of Kindness. The key psalm thus says, "Appoint mercy and truth that they may preserve it" (Psalms 61:8).

Toward the end of the day. At the end of the day, a person must be highly motivated, thinking of how the Heart and the Spring take leave of each other and sing to each other. The creation of that day is over, and who knows what the next day will bring? Therefore, at this time, one must prepare oneself to accept the holiness of the next day (*Likutey Etzoth* B, *Tefillah* 25).

take leave... *Gezegen.*

lyrics. *Luder* in Yiddish. This is alluded to in the key psalm, "I will sing praise to Your name forever, so that I will daily keep my vows" (Psalms 61:9). The days that the Heart gives the Spring come from these songs and hymns (end of story).

The True Man of Kindness watches very carefully over this. At the exact end of the day, the True Man of Kindness gives the Heart a gift of one day.* The Heart gives the day to the Spring, and the Spring then once again has time.

When this day comes from the place from which it comes, it also comes with very wonderful parables and lyrics containing all types of wisdom.*

There are differences between the various days.* There is Sunday, Monday, etc.... Besides this, there are New Moon days and festivals.

All the time that the True Man of Kindness has comes from my hand. It is I who go forth and gather all the true kindness, from which time comes into existence.*

Time is produced by song. Thus, the seven voices in Psalm 29 parallel the seven days of creation. The voices of song are the source of time (*Likutey Halakhoth, Rosh HaShanah* 5:9). In this story, the third, fourth, and sixth beggars have their power through song (*Likutey Halakhoth, Apitropos* 3:4).

The daily song of the Heart and Spring parallel the song of the Levites sung in the Holy Temple. These songs contain great wisdom, as it is written, "Sing O wise one" (Psalms 47:8). It is also written, "Hezekiah spoke to the Levites who have good intelligence toward God" (2 Chronicles, 30:22). Rashi comments that the song of the Levites is referred to as intelligence and wisdom (*Zimrath HaAretz*).

gift of one day. It is therefore written in the key psalm, "May You add to the days of the King" (Psalms 61:7).

all types of wisdom. Thus, the third beggar had access to all sorts of wisdom. The wisdom of all the other men involved something from something, while the wisdom of the Torah involves something from nothing. The others could find metals in the ground and combine various substances, but this is all something from something. But "Wisdom comes from Nothingness, and where is the place of Understanding?" (Job 28:12). Wisdom and understanding of the Torah come from Nothingness, and from it, one can understand how God brought the creation forth from Nothingness.

The third beggar was on the level of perceiving this. The other men knew how to find various metals, but he knew the songs that were the source of time, and hence the source of all wisdom (*Likutey Halakhoth, Keriyath HaTorah* 6:36).

between the various days. This is discussed in detail in the writings of the Ari (see *Etz Chaim, Drush Egolim VeYoshar* 5, p. 43). Since every day is different, one must praise God with different songs, and with an entirely new mentality, each day (*Likutey Etzoth* B, *Tefillah* 25). It goes without saying that during the month of Elul and on Rosh HaShanah one must worship God with new praise (*Rimzey Maasioth*).

existence. Thus the Heart only exists because it can look at the Spring, and because of the Heart, the rest of world can exist. But both the Heart and Spring only exist because

(It is for this reason that he is wiser even than the wise man who is as wise as any day one prefers. This is because time and days come into existence primarily through the beggar with a speech defect, who gathers true kindness, which is the basis of time, and brings this kindness to the True Man of Kindness. The latter gives a day to the Heart, who in turn gives it to the Spring, and as a result, the entire world is sustained. Therefore, time is brought into existence with parables and lyrics that contain all wisdom, through the beggar with the speech defect.)

Therefore, I have the word of the True Man of Kindness that I can recite parables and lyrics that contain all wisdom. All time, along with parables and lyrics, comes into existence through my hand.

And now, I am giving you this as a wedding present. You should be just like me.

After he gave them this blessing there was great joy and rejoicing.

The Fourth Day*

They completed the celebration of that day, and went to sleep. The next morning, the couple began to yearn for the beggar with the crooked neck.

All at once, he appeared and said: Here I am... Originally, I blessed you that you should be like me. Now I am giving you this as a wedding present.

You think I have a crooked neck.* Actually, my neck is not crooked at all. Quite the contrary, I have a very straight neck. I have a very beautiful neck.*

---

of the stutterer (who perfected the concept of speech), who gathers all Chesed-kindness, and weaves it into time (*Likutey Halakhoth, Melamdim* 4:13).

The Fourth Day. Rabbi Nachman told this part of the story on the same Friday night as he told about the third day. He finished telling the story of the fourth day, and then quickly left the table (*Sichoth HaRan* 151).

crooked neck. The neck involves the sefiroth of Binah and Tifereth (*Kedushath Shabbath*).

In the writings of the Ari, however, the neck is not seen as a sefirah, but as a manifestation of "immature mentality" (*mochin de-katnuth*).

In order to produce the perfect sound, his neck had to be crooked, just as a shofar must be bent (see *Rosh HaShanah* 16b).

beautiful neck. This is alluded to in the verse, "Your neck is like the tower of David, built

However, there are vapors* in the world. I do not want to exhale and add to the vain vapors* of the world. It is for this reason that my neck appears to be crooked. I made my neck crooked to avoid exhaling into the vapors of the world. But actually, I have a very beautiful, wonderful neck, since I have a wonderful voice.* There are many sounds in the world that do not involve speech. I have such a wonderful neck and voice that I can mimic any of these sounds.

Regarding this I have the word* of the land of music. There is a land where everyone is expert in the science of music. Everyone there studies this discipline, even little children. There is no child there who cannot play some kind of musical instrument. The least person in this

with turrets, upon which hang a thousand shields, the armor of mighty warriors" (Song of Songs 4:4).

The tzaddik thus has a wonderful neck (*Likutey Etzoth* B, *Tzaddik* 93). The neck also alludes to the Temple. We thus find that when Joseph fell on Benjamin's neck, our sages state that this alluded to the destruction of the two Temples (*Zimrath HaAretz*).

vapors. The Hebrew word is *hevel*, which denotes both vapor or breath and vanity (see Ecclesiastes 1:2). *Dukh* in Yiddish. Here too the beggar was so removed from the worldly that he did not want to leave any breath in this physical world (*Likutey Halakhoth, Choshen Mishpat, HaOseh Sheliach LiGboth Chovo* 2:10, p. 82a).

add to the vain vapors. This beggar boasted that he would not let any worldly vapor come into his throat; therefore, his neck appeared crooked. As a result, he had perfection. This is like the shofar, which is crooked and is the root of all sound. The shofar is related to the Future World, and the sefirah of Binah. It is thus written, "On that day, the great shofar will be sounded" (Isaiah 27:13). When this beggar makes his neck crooked so that no worldly vanities can enter his body, he exists totally in the World to Come.

The "vapors" or *hevel* of the shofar is that which is mentioned in the verse, "Vapor of vapors, says Koheleth, vapor of vapors, all is vapor" (Ecclesiastes 1:2; see *Tikkuney Zohar*. The word *vapor* (*hevel*) is mentioned five times in this verse, alluding to the spiritual vapors or breaths on all five levels of creation (see *Sefer Yetzirah* 1:5).

Rosh HaShanah is the first of the Ten Days of Repentance. On Rosh HaShanah we sound the shofar indicating that we must cast away all worldliness and live completely for the World to Come (*Likutey Halakhoth, Nedarim* 4:36).

voice. The previous beggar had perfected speech. This one perfected voice, which is more spiritual than speech. Kabbalistically, speech pertains to Malkhuth, while voice pertains to the six sefiroth of Zer Anpin.

The root of all voice is the seven voices mentioned in Psalm 29 (*Kedushath Shabbath*).

word. *Haskamah,* that is "agreement," as above.

land would be the greatest musician any place else. The wise men there, as well as the king and the musicians, are extraordinarily skilled in this art.

Once the leading sages of that land sat down, and each one boasted about his music.* One boasted about his skill on one instrument, while another boasted about his skill on another instrument. One boasted how well he played one instrument, and another boasted that he could play several instruments. Still another one boasted that he was able to play all musical instruments.

Another one then boasted that he could mimic a certain musical instrument with his voice. Still another boasted that he could mimic a different instrument. Yet another boasted that he knew how to mimic many instruments. Another boasted that he could mimic the beating of a drum so well that it sounded exactly like a drum.* Another boasted that with his voice he could mimic the sound of artillery.*

I was also there. I spoke up and said to them, "My voice is better than your voices. This is proof. If you are so skilled in music, let us see if you can help the two lands.

"There are two lands which are a thousand miles apart.* At night, people in these two lands cannot sleep. As soon as night falls, everyone—men, women and children—begins to wail. If a stone were placed there, it would melt out of pity for this wailing. They hear a great sound of sobbing,* and because of this, all the men, women and children wail. This is true in both lands. The same sound of sobbing is heard in both lands, even though these two lands are a thousand miles apart.

"If you are so skilled in music, I would like to see if you can help

music. *Muzika* in Yiddish. In this story, the third, fourth, and sixth days speak of song (*Likutey Halakhoth, Apitropos* 3:4).

drum. *Poik* in Yiddish.

artillery. *K'neh s'refah* in Hebrew, literally "burning cane"; *irmatis* in Yiddish.

a thousand miles apart. Some say this is the distance between Uman and Jerusalem.

sobbing. *Yelalah* in Hebrew. It is noteworthy that the word *yelalah* has the same letters as *laylah*, meaning "night." The wailing is hence related to the blemish of the moon (*Chokhmah U'Tevunah* 9:3).

these two lands, or if you can mimic their sound. Let's see if you reproduce the exact sound of the wailing that is heard there."

The wise men said to me,* "Will you bring us there?"

"Yes, I will," I* replied.

They all set out, and eventually came to one of the two lands. At
night, when everyone began to wail, the wise men also began to wail.
It was quite obvious that they could do nothing to help these people.

"In any case," I said to the wise men, "tell me what is the source
of the sobbing that is heard here."

"And you *do* know!" they replied.

"I most certainly do," I said. "There are two birds,* one male and
one female. They are the only such pair of birds in the world. The

---

to me. The story uses the third person, "to him." It often switches between the third and
first persons.

I. "He" in the text.

two birds. The two birds allude to God (Zer Anpin) and the Shekhinah (Malkhuth). The concept of Rosh HaShanah and Yom Kippur is to bring Malkhuth (the feminine aspect of the
Divine) face to face with Zer Anpin (the male aspect of the Divine), so that the unification can be complete. This is the concept of uniting "those who dwell on high and
those who dwell below," the "Holy One Blessed be He," and His Shekhinah. The "Holy
One" is called "Heaven," while the Shekhinah is called "Earth." It is thus written, "God
founded the Earth with wisdom, and established the Heaven with understanding"
(Proverbs 3:19). It is our task to reunite Heaven and Earth, the Holy One and His Shekhinah (*Likutey Halakhoth, Nedarim* 4:24).

The fact that the two birds are lost to each other alludes to the exile of the Shekhinah.
The exiled Shekhinah is referred to as "a bird who has wandered from its nest" (Proverbs
27:8). The verse continues, "so is a man who wanders from his place." The "Man" in
this verse is the Holy One (*Tikkuney Zohar*).

The two birds also parallel the two cherubs on the ark. When the Temple existed, the
cherubs were face to face, but when it was destroyed, they were lost to each other and
were back to back.

The Shekhinah is also referred to as the "Congregation of Israel," since it is the Divine
Presence that rests on each and every Israelite. It is our task to bring it back to its root
in God. The tzaddik can accomplish this by throwing his voice, as we shall see (*Likutey
Halakhoth, Nedarim* 4:25).

The shofar includes the sounds of the two birds, the sound from "on high" and the
sound from "down below." It thus serves to reunite God and His Shekhinah (ibid.).

The two cherubs were the source of prophecy, as it is written, "Moses heard the Voice
from between the two cherubs" (Numbers 7:89). The voice of prophecy is also related

female was lost, and the male went to look for her. He searched for her, and She searched for him. They searched for one another for a very long time, until they got completely lost.

"When they realized that they could not find one another, they decided to remain where they were and build themselves nests. The male bird made himself a nest near one of the two lands. He was not right next to the land, but he was close enough that the people of the land could hear his voice from the place where he built his nest.*

to the shofar, as it is written, "Lift up your voice like a shofar" (Isaiah 58:1). It is also written, "Your mouth is like a shofar" (Hosea 8:1).

At the revelation at Sinai, the Torah thus says, "The sound of the shofar became continually stronger, Moses spoke and God answered in a voice" (Exodus 19:19). The sound of the shofar indicated that all the Israelites were reaching a level of prophecy. Rashi also notes that God made Moses' voice stronger. This was done through the sound of the shofar (ibid.).

The two cherubs from which prophecy came denote the Holy One and His Shekhinah. As long as the ark with the cherubs stood in the Temple, the relationship between the Holy One and the Shekhinah was perfect, and prophecy could exist. However, after the Temple was destroyed, and the ark hidden, prophecy ceased to exist (*Likutey Halakhoth, Nedarim* 4:36).

The concept of bringing together the two birds is thus that of reuniting the Holy One and His Shekhinah, which is the redemption (*Rimzey Maasioth*).

The wailing of these birds is alluded to in the verse, "God cries out from on high. He screams from His Holy Habitation" (Jeremiah 25:30). The Talmud states that He cries out like a dove (*Berakhoth* 3a). The Shekhinah is represented by Rachel, regarding which it is written, "A voice is heard in Ramah, lamentation and weeping, Rachel weeping for her children. She refuses to be comforted for her children, because they are not there" (Jeremiah 31:15) (*Likutey Etzoth* B, *Tzaddik* 93).

The two birds were a perfect pair. This is alluded to where the verse refers to the Shekhinah as "my dove, my twin" (Song of Songs 5:2, 6:9). This indicates that God and Israel are like twin birds. Regarding their mutual loss, it is written, "My beloved passed by ... I sought Him, but could not find Him" (Song of Songs 5:6). When the Temple was destroyed, the two birds were lost to each other. When it is rebuilt, they will be reunited (*Chokhmah U'Tevunah* 19:3).

Rabbi Nachman also speaks of the "birds" as being the source of voice and the rectification of malicious speech (*Likutey Moharan* 3). Malicious speech separated the birds, and therefore their rectification is through voice. David became the "shepherd of Israel" because he was worthy of rectifying the song of holiness by writing the Psalms (ibid.).

nest. This is alluded to in the verse, "My soul yearns and pines for God's courtyards, my heart and flesh sing to the living God. A bird has found a house, and the swallow a nest for herself" (Psalms 85:3, 4).

"The female bird built her nest near the other land. She too was close enough that they could hear her voice. At night, both of these birds begin to wail in a very loud voice. Each one wails for its mate. It is this sound of wailing that is heard in these two lands. When the people hear this wailing, they too all begin to wail. Therefore, they cannot sleep."

The wise men did not want to believe me. "Will you bring us there?" they asked.

"Yes," I replied. "I can bring you there. But you will not be able to come there. If you come close, you will not be able to tolerate the sound of the wailing. Even here, you cannot stand it, and you are forced to wail along with the others. If you were there, you would not be able to stand it at all.

"It is also impossible to come there by day, since it is impossible to tolerate the joy that is there. By day, birds gather around each one of the pair, and they console each one and make it extremely joyful. The birds speak words of consolation, telling the pair that there is still a possibility that they will find one another.

"Therefore, during the day, it is impossible to tolerate the great joy that exists there. The sound of the birds who make them rejoice cannot be heard from a great distance, only when one is actually there. However, the sound of the pair's wailing at night can be heard at a very great distance. Because of all this, it is impossible to approach their place."

"Can you rectify this?" they asked me.

I replied, "I can rectify this, since I can mimic any sound* in the world. With my voice I can reproduce any sound exactly. Besides this,

The *Zohar* also relates the Shekhinah to a bird in its nest in the commandment telling that when a bird is found on its nest, the mother must be sent away before the young can be taken (*Likutey Halakhoth, Nedarim* 4:25).

mimic any sound. The tzaddik must be able to mimic every sound in the world, thus elevating every sound according to its time and place. This is also related to the concept of sounding the shofar on Rosh HaShanah. The shofar includes every sound in the world, as the *Zohar* teaches, "All sounds on high are included in the shofar" (*Zohar* 2:99b; cf. *Zohar* 3:18b).

The shofar is directed at both birds, alluding to God and Israel. The shofar awakens the Israelites and motivates them to repent, saying to them, "Awake, you who sleep." This

I can also throw my voice,* so that no sound is heard here, but the sound is heard at a distance. I can therefore throw the voice of the female bird and make it reach the place of the male bird, and also throw the voice of the male bird and make it reach the place of the female bird. By doing this, I will be able to bring them together. Through this, everything will be rectified."

When he saw* that they did not believe him, he took them into a forest. They heard the sound of a door being opened, and then closed

is the concept of, "Shall a shofar be sounded and the people not tremble?" (Amos 3:6). The shofar also serves to remind God to have mercy on us. It recalls the binding of Isaac on the altar and causes God to remember his merit for us.

Thus, the shofar tends to bring Israel to God, and God to Israel. Symbolically, then, it reunites the two birds (*Likutey Halakhoth*, *Nedarim* 4:25).

throw my voice. The tzaddik can bring God and the Shekhinah together by throwing his voice. One way of doing this is by clothing his lessons in stories. The message is not heard immediately, but when it reaches the person for whom it is intended, it is heard well. Telling stories is therefore throwing one's voice at the Israelites.

The tzaddik can also clothe his prayers in stories. Because of spiritual barriers, he cannot make such prayers directly, and to all practical purposes they seem like stories. But in the place where they are needed, they are heard. In this respect, he is throwing his voice toward God (cf. *Likutey Moharan* 5).

Sounding the shofar is also throwing a voice toward Israel and toward God (*Likutey Halakhoth*, *Nedarim* 4:24).

Moses was a tzaddik who could throw his voice so that the Israelites heard it wherever they were. Through the sound of the shofar, God helped make his voice powerful so that even those furthest away could hear him. The Torah describes the sound of the shofar as being "very (*m'od*) strong" (Exodus 19:16). The word very (*m'od*) is interpreted in the Midrash as denoting death (*Bereshith Rabbah* 9:10). Therefore, Moses' voice, as enhanced by the shofar, could even arouse those who were so evil that they would be considered dead (*Likutey Halakhoth*, *Nedarim* 4:25).

The concept of the voice from the cherubs was also that of throwing the voice. Therefore, the prophet Samuel could hear the voice, but Eli, who was closer, could not hear it (see 1 Samuel, 3:4, Rashi ad loc.) (*Likutey Halakhoth*, *Nedarim* 4:36).

The concept of throwing the voice is also that of the tzaddik who can tell one person something and not have it have any effect on him, but it can have an effect on other people. Rabbi Nachman thus said, "I tell you something, and sometimes it will not affect you at all. But the words are passed from person to person, from one friend to another. These words finally reach a particular individual and penetrate deeply into his heart. The words then fulfill their mission and inspire him..." (*Sichoth HaRan* 208).

when he saw... Literally, "But who will believe this?"

and locked with a bolt. They actually heard the click* of the bolt. Then they heard a gun* being shot, and a dog being sent to retrieve the quarry. The dog thrashed* around and dragged himself in the snow.*

The wise men heard all this, but they did not see a thing. They also did not hear any sound whatsoever coming from me. Still, I* was the one who was projecting these sounds, and this is why they heard them. They realized that I could accurately produce any sound and also throw my voice. Therefore, I could rectify everything.*

(Rabbi Nachman did not tell any more about this, and it is understood that he skipped part of the story* here.)

Therefore, I have the word of that land that I have a wonderful voice, and that I can mimic any sound in the world. Now, as a wedding present, I am giving it to you, so that you will be like me.

When he completed his story there was very great joy and rejoicing there.

---

click. *Klainka* in Yiddish.

gun. *Biks.*

thrashed. *Mith-chabet* in Hebrew.

dragged himself in the snow. *Gegraznit in shnai* in Yiddish. The dog retrieving his quarry alludes to Esau who brought game back to his father (Genesis 27:30). Esau is likened to a dog (*Zohar* 3:124b; *Likutey Halakhoth, Nedarim* 4:24, end).
This shows that this beggar could even throw his voice with regard to mundane matters. Since he could do this, he obviously could do the same with regard to holy matters, and thus reunite the birds (*Rimzey Maasioth*).

I. Literally "the one with the crooked neck." For consistency, we have changed it to the first person.

rectify everything. Since the tzaddik has the voice of the two birds, he can unite them. The shofar is also the spirit-wind of prophecy that comes from the cherubs (birds). Therefore, the shofar will gather the exile (Isaiah 27:13). The gathering of the exile depends primarily on reuniting the birds (*Likutey Halakhoth, Nedarim* 4:36).

skipped part of the story. Rabbi Nachman did not complete the story, since he would not reveal how the redemption was to take place. The redemption, furthermore, depends on all the world repenting. Thus the redemption can only come in its proper time. But, once the others accepted the fact that he can accomplish it, the redemption will automatically come (*Rimzey Maasioth*).

The Fifth Day*
On the fifth day, while they were rejoicing, the couple recalled the hunchback beggar. They yearned for him very much, saying, "How can we bring the hunchback beggar here? If he were here, there would be very great joy."*

Suddenly he appeared and said, "Here I am! I have come to the wedding." With that, he fell on them, hugging and kissing them.

He then said to them: Originally, I blessed you that you should be like I am. Now I am giving you this as a wedding present—that you should be like me.

I am not a hunchback* at all. Quite the contrary, I have broad shoulders.* My shoulders are a case of "little holding much."* I have

The Fifth Day. Rabbi Nachman told the story of the fifth day on the next Sunday (April 8) (*Sichoth HaRan* 149). Rabbi Nachman was involved in a discussion of a certain cult (*kat*), and spoke about having "broad shoulders" (*breita pleitzes*) to be able to assume responsibility. This led to his telling the story of the fifth day (*Sichoth HaRan* 151; *Chayay Moharan* 16b 5).

very great joy. It is only with respect to this beggar that this expression is used. Rabbi Nachman told this part of the story in great joy (*Chayay Moharan* 16b 5).

hunchback. He appeared to be a hunchback because he bent his body to accept the yoke of the Torah. He therefore never straightened out his body, which would involve throwing off this yoke. He was like Issachar, regarding whom it is said, "He bent his shoulder to the burden" (Genesis 49:15). This was also the level of the sons of Kehoth, who carried the ark and tablets on their shoulders. If one carries the Torah, one can carry all things, since the ark supported its carriers. This is because the Torah is related to the level that existed before God created space (*Likutey Halakhoth, Sefer Torah* 3:7).

broad shoulders. *Pleitzes* in Yiddish. The expression *breita pleitzes*, or "broad shoulders," denotes the ability to take on large responsibilities, especially with regard to doctrinal matters. A hunchback, on the other hand, appears to have no shoulders at all. Therefore, this beggar was saying that his "nonexistent" shoulders were really very broad, since they were "little holding much."

little holding much. *Muat machzik eth ha-merubah* in Hebrew. This expression occurs in the Midrash (*Bereshith Rabbah* 95). The concept is found in many other places as well (see *Bereshith Rabbah* 5:6; *Vayikra Rabbah* 10:9; Rashi on Leviticus 8:3). It is taught that such a phenomenon occurred among the Israelites on seven occasions (*ibid., Maaseh Torah* 118).

In general, the concept of "little holding much" is that of transcending space. There are various levels of this, until one reaches the level where space is transcended completely (*Likutey Halakhoth, Tzitzith* 3:8). Sin brings a person under the realm of space. We thus find that after Cain killed Abel, he was condemned to be a "wanderer and a

an affidavit* regarding this.

Once there was a discussion, where people were boasting about this concept. Each one boasted that he was a case of little holding much. Everyone laughed at one of them and made a joke of him, but the others who boasted about being little holding much were accepted. However, in my case, the concept of little holding much is greater than that of all of them.

One of these people boasted that his brain was an example of little holding much. In his brain, he carried thousands and myriads of people, with all their needs, all their habits, all their discussions,* and all their movements. Since his brain carried so many* people, it was an example of little holding much.

The others laughed at him. They said that the people are nothing, and therefore he is also nothing.*

One spoke up and said, "I saw such a case of little holding much. I once saw a mountain which was covered with excrement and filth. I found it very surprising, and I wondered where all this excrement and filth came from."

"There was a man near the mountain, and he said, 'All this came from me.' That man lived near the mountain, and whenever he ate

---

fugitive" (Genesis 4:12; *Likutey Halakhoth, Tzitzith* 3:14).

The concept of "little holding much" applies to the Land of Israel as a whole. It is called "land of the deer," because like a deerskin it can "stretch" to hold all its inhabitants. The Hebrew language is also "little holding much," since a few words can hold many mysteries (*Zimrath HaAretz*).

affidavit. *Haskamah.* See above p. 13.

discussions. *Havayoth,* in both in Hebrew and Yiddish. The word can denote "existences," but it also denotes arguments or discussions (see *Sukkah* 28a; *Bava Bathra* 134a).

brain carried so many. A person might boast that he is a great man because he has responsibilities for his family and household. But we see that even one who has responsibility for thousands is not so great, because it is all for vanity and nothingness (*Rimzey Maasioth*).

There are seven levels of people discussed here. These might parallel the seven cases where "little held much" mentioned in the Midrash (*Bereshith Rabbah* 5:6; see above).

he is also nothing. A person can boast that he sustains thousands of people, but what he gives them is physical, and therefore worthless, so his accomplishment is nothing (*Likutey Etzoth* B, *Tzaddik* 94).

and drank, he would throw his garbage and excrement there. He therefore made it a filthy place, putting a large amount of garbage and excrement on the mountain. Therefore, this man was an example of little holding much, since he was able to produce so much excrement.

"This is the same concept* as that of the man who boasted that his brain held many people."

One boasted that he was an example of little holding much. He had an estate that produced much fruit. When the amount of fruit produced by the land was calculated, it came out that the land did not have enough room to hold all the fruit. There was not enough space in the land to hold all the fruit that it produced. Therefore, it was an example of little holding much.

His words were well accepted.* This was considered an excellent example of little holding much.

One said that he had a very wonderful orchard containing fruit. It was such a beautiful orchard that many people and nobles traveled there. In the summer, many people and nobles would come there to take walks. The orchard, however, did not have room for all the people who came there, so it was an example of little holding much.

His words were also well accepted.

One said that his speech was an example of little holding much. He was the secretary* for a great king, and many people came to him. Some came with praise for the king, while others came with petitions. "It is obviously impossible for the king to hear them all," he said, "so I take all their messages and condense them into a few words that I tell the king. The few short words of mine contain all their praises and petitions. Therefore my speech is little holding much."

One said that his silence was an example of little holding much.

---

the same concept. Rabbi Nachman is speaking here about an unworthy leader. He may have responsibility for thousands of people, but he ruins the souls of those who follow him (see *Likutey Moharan Tinyana* 8:8). What he gives to his followers is like the excrement that the man here spreads around the mountain, and then boasts that it is all from him (*Rimzey Maasioth*).

His words were well accepted. Because he actually produced fruit. Thus, he was a great tzaddik, who had the concept of little holding much (*Likutey Etzoth* B, *Tzaddik* 94).

secretary. *Sekretar* in Yiddish.

Many people were denouncing him and slandering him very much, but no matter how much they did so, he would answer them all with silence. Throughout it all, he remained completely silent. His silence was an answer for everything. Therefore his silence was little holding much.

One said that he was an example of little holding much. He explained, "There is a man who is poor and blind, and also very huge. I, on the other hand, am very small. But even though I am very small, I lead the poor blind man, who is very huge. Therefore, I am little holding much. The blind man could trip and fall, but by leading him, I am actually 'holding' him up.* Therefore, I am a little 'holding' much. I am little, but I uphold this huge man."

I was also there, and I said, "Actually, you are all examples of little holding much. I understand the true meaning of everything that you said. I know what you truly mean when you boast of being examples of little holding much. The last of you, who boasted that he leads a blind man, is the greatest of you all. But I am much higher than any of you.

"When the last one boasted that he led a giant, he meant that he directed the orbit* of the moon. The moon is considered to be a blind man, since it does not have any of its own light, and has nothing of its own.* Although this boaster is small, he directs the moon, which is

'holding' him up. In Hebrew this is also *machzik.* Thus it is "little holding much."

orbit. Literally, "leads the sphere of the moon."

nothing of its own. *Leyth lah le-garmei klum* in Aramaic. The expression is from the *Zohar* (1:238a, 1:249b). The moon is therefore also considered a "poor man." In this respect, the moon is also seen as an aspect of Malkhuth, which "has nothing of its own" (see *Likutey Moharan* 1).

The succession of concepts of "the little that holds much" that are introduced here alludes to successive levels of *teshuva*, repentance.

Rabbi Nachman explains that *teshuva* is the path to Kether, the crown, the glory of God. To achieve this, a person must set aside his own honor, and the way to do this is through being silent. This means the ability to hear himself abused and still say nothing.

The different aspects of *teshuva* are expressed in the form of the letter *aleph.* The letter is made up of an upper point, a lower point, and a line, which both connects and divides the two points. The lower point of the *aleph*, the *chirik*, alludes to remaining silent. The upper point refers to *Kether*, the concealed throne of God's glory. The *vav* is the *rakiya*, the firmament of many colors, an allusion to *busha*, shame—the shame of one

very large. Moreover, he sustains the entire world, since the world needs the moon. Therefore, he is actually a true example of little holding much."

Nevertheless, my concept of little holding much is much greater than all, including his. This is the proof:

Once there was a group of people who studied the fact that every animal has a shadow in which it likes to rest. Conversely, there is a shadow for each and every animal. Every animal chooses its particular shadow where it wants to dwell.

Every bird, also, has its own unique branch. It is on this particular branch that it desires to live.

Studying this phenomenon, they sought to find a tree* in whose

who comes before his Maker after sinning (for the face of one who is embarrassed changes color) (*Bava Metzia* 58b).

When all these levels are brought together (by a person's attaining them), there is "unity between the sun and the moon": the sun (of divine wisdom) shines to the receiving moon. This idea corresponds to the unity between Moses and his disciple, Joshua. For "the face of Moses is like the face of the sun" (*Baba Bathra* 75a)—and Moses is the upper point of the *aleph*. The face of Joshua is like the face of the moon (for all his knowledge was derived from Moses)—and Joshua is the lower point of the *aleph*. Moses and Joshua are united by means of the tent, the stretched-out firmament as it were, for "Joshua the son of Nun did not move from the tent" (Exodus 33:11).

These three levels also correspond to the three *mitzvoth* that Israel was commanded to fulfill upon entering the Land of Israel. The first was to wipe out Amalek. This mitzvah was particularly associated with Joshua because he had been instructed by Moses to go out and fight Amalek (Exodus 17:9). The second mitzvah was to build the Holy Temple. This is associated with Moses, who built the sanctuary. The third mitzvah was to appoint a king. This corresponds to the level of the firmament, as it is written, "A star shall step forth out of Jacob" (Numbers 24:17), referring to the king of Israel (Rashi ad loc.). So too is Jacob, who "dwelled in tents" (Gen. 25:27) (*Likutey Moharan* 6).

In the story we also find these three points. First there is the level of silence, referring to Joshua and corresponding to the lower point of the *aleph*. Next mentioned is the man leading the blind pauper, that is, he is above the moon and is the one to bring it its needs, corresponding to the *vav*. The third level is the one who is higher than this firmament, the upper point of the *aleph*, the hunchback himself. He corresponds to the level of Moses, and he himself has the aspect of "the little that holds much," the Holy Temple. (Rabbi Chaim Kramer).

tree. This tree is alluded to in Daniel's vision: "I saw a tree in the middle of the world, and it was very high. The tree grew and was strong, and it was so high that it reached the heavens. Its view was to the end of the earth. Its leaves were beautiful, and it had much fruit, providing food for all. The beasts of the field had shadow under it, and the shadow all animals live.* All animals would desire to live in its shadow. Similarly, all birds* would live in its branches.

They probed and discovered that such a tree exists. They wanted to go to the tree, since near it there is wonderful delight* that is beyond

birds of heaven lived on its branches; all living things had food from it" (Daniel 4:7–9). This tree is the Tree of Life, which was in the Garden of Eden (Genesis 2:9). Since all animals can live under this tree, it is an example of "little holding much." This tree is the link between space and the realm that is above space. It is through the Tree of Life that souls can travel from the world, which is the realm of space, to the Throne of Glory, which is above space.

If Adam had not sinned, he would have entered into the realm of "above space" during his lifetime. This is the concept of "knowledge." But, "Adam who is in honor understands it not; he is like the beasts who perish" (Psalms 49:21). By sinning, he lost the concept of "knowledge," and was lowered into the concept of space. The rectification for this is through repentance, which "reaches up to the Throne of Glory" (Yoma 86b). In the time of the Temple, repentance was often accompanied by a sacrifice. The sacrifice related to the animal's place under the tree, and hence brought a person into contact with the tree. The person would then be raised to the level above space (Likutey Halakhoth, Tzitzith 3:13).

The Tree of Life is the joy of the World to Come. It is above the concept of space, since it is where souls go up to delight in God.

The Tree of Life is the root of the Torah, which is called, "The Tree of Life to those who grasp onto it" (Proverbs 3:18). One can only approach this tree through the "path to the Tree of Life" (Genesis 3:24). The path is the commandments of the Torah, which are called a "path" (Deuteronomy 5:30) (Likutey Halakhoth, Sefer Torah 3:2).

Since the Torah is related to the tree which is above space, the ark which stood in the Temple and held the original Torah and tablets did not take up any space. If one measured from the walls to the ark, it would come out that the ark did not take up any space at all (Bava Bathra 99a; Yoma 21a; Likutey Halakhoth, Sefer Torah 3:6).

It is taught that "all souls come through the great tree" (Zohar). The Tree of Life stands under the Throne of Glory, and all souls go up on it (Likutey Halakhoth, Choshen Mishpat, Sheluchim 4:16).

The tree also represents the bush in which the ram substituted for Isaac was captured (Genesis 22:13). From this ram's horn, the shofar was made. The sounds of the shofar allude to the four concepts of the tree, as we shall see (ibid.).

all animals live. Since there is room for all animals and birds on this tree, it is above space (Chokhmah U'Tevunah 20:2).

birds. Literally, "birds of heaven." In Hebrew it is tziparey shmaya, the term that occurs in Daniel 4:9. (Also see Ezekiel 31:13.)

delight. This is because the tree denotes the delight of the World to Come, the interface between the physical world, which is spacial, and the spiritual world, which is nonall imagination. All birds and animals are there, and none harms the other. They all live in harmony and frolic together, so it must be an extraordinary delight to be near that tree.

They then probed to discover which direction they must travel to reach the tree. A dispute* arose regarding this, and none of them could come to a conclusion. Some said that they should head east, while others said that it was to the west. One determined that the tree must be in one place, while another said that it was elsewhere. Thus, they could not decide which way to go to come to the tree.

spacial (*Likutey Halakhoth, Yoreh Deah, Sefer Torah* 3:2; see *Likutey Etzoth B, Tzaddik* 99).

dispute. This too is caused by sin. After mankind sinned, the path to the Tree of Life was no longer revealed to all.

The breaking of the tablets also caused forgetting, so that there is no longer any clear path to the tree. This brings about disputes between the sages. Even in the time of the Talmud, such disputes existed. But all disputes come about because people do not have the roots of the tree, which are the roots of Torah, that is, faith, reverence, humility and truth (*Likutey Halakhoth, Sefer Torah* 3:1).

God also planted a burning revolving sword along the way to guard the path to the Tree of Life (Genesis 3:24). Because of this sword we do not know where this tree is. There is therefore a dispute as to which direction to take to the tree, and from this all the disputes in the world originate.

Sometimes the motivation behind a dispute can be holy, such as the disputes between Talmudic sages. But at other times, the motivations can be unworthy, and the disputes can lead to causeless hatred. It was such hatred that caused the Temple to be destroyed (*Yoma* 9b). All this comes from the sword, which is a symbol of strife and war.

The sword is therefore described as *mith-hapekheth* which means turning, revolving, or transforming. It is taught that it is called "transforming," because it transforms one opinion into another, causing dispute (*Zohar* 1:121a). This sword came about as a result of Adam's sin.

In the Future World, "The days of My people will be like the days of a tree" (Isaiah 65:22). Strife will no longer exist, even in the animal kingdom, since "the wolf will lie with the lamb..." (Isaiah 11:6). The sword will be rectified, since "people will beat their swords into plowshares" (Isaiah 2:4). This is through the power of the tree, regarding which, it is said, "It is a Tree of Life to those who grasp on to it ... and all its paths are peace" (Proverbs 3:18) (*Likutey Halakhoth, Sefer Torah* 3:10).

The main concept of dispute arises because of the concept of space. Dispute arises when one party wishes to enter the space or territory of another. But on the level above space, there is no dispute. It is thus taught, "When our love was strong, we found enough room to sleep together on the side of a sword" (*Sanhedrin* 7a). This was the rectification of the "revolving sword" (*Likutey Halakhoth, Sefer Torah* 3:11).

Then a wise man came and said to them, "Why are you trying to discover in which direction the tree lies? Instead, try to find out who will be able to approach the tree. Not everyone can come near it. In order to do so, one must have all the attributes* of the tree. The tree has three roots. The first root is faith,* the second reverence,* and the third, humility.* The trunk of the tree is truth,* and it is from there

attributes. *Middoth.*

faith. *Emunah.*

reverence. *Yirah.* Also translated as "fear," as in "fear of heaven." It denotes the awe of God, as well as the fear of divine retribution.

humility. *Anivuth.*

truth. The Tree represents the Torah, but the five books of the Torah are paralleled by the five books of the Psalms. The Psalms begin by speaking of the path and the tree.

The Psalms begin, "Happy is the man who does not walk in the counsel of the wicked" (Psalms 1:1). This parallels the attribute of faith, since faith comes from the advice of the tzaddik (*Likutey Moharan* 7; *Likutey Moharan Tinyana* 5). One who does not walk in the ways of the wicked will follow the advice of the tzaddik, and will thus gain faith. "Who does not stand in the path of sinners" denotes reverence and fear of God. Fear is the antithesis of sin, as it is written, "that His God's fear be on your faces that you do not sin" (Exodus 20:20). An important trait is "fear of sin." "Who does not sit in the place of scorners," denotes humility. It is thus written, "If he goes to scorners, then he will scorn, but to the humble he gives grace" (Proverbs 3:34). We therefore see that humility is the antithesis of scoffing and scorning. Scoffing comes from the sin of pride. "But who desires God's Torah, and immerses himself in it day and night" (Psalms 1:1) denotes the tree itself, which is truth.

The psalm goes on, "He shall be like a tree planted by the streams of water" (Psalms 1:3). This denotes the tree in the story, planted by the supernal streams, regarding which it is written, "God's streams are filled with water" (Psalms 65:10) (*Likutey Halakhoth, Sefer Torah* 3:3).

The four attributes of the tree also represent Abraham, Isaac, Jacob, and Moses.

Abraham represents faith, as it is written, "He had faith in God" (Genesis 15:6).

Isaac represents reverence and fear; hence, God is referred to as "the feared of Isaac" (Genesis 31:53).

Jacob represents truth, which is the trunk of the tree, as it is written, "You will give truth to Jacob" (Micah 7:20). This is the body of the Torah, which is referred to as "the Torah of truth" (Malachi 2:6). It is written, "Moses commanded us the Torah, an inheritance of the congregation of *Jacob*" (Deuteronomy 33:4). The Ari teaches that Jacob represented the Torah, but since the trait of humility was not perfected, it could not be given until Moses arrived on the scene.

Moses represents humility, as it is written, "Moses was humble, more so than any man

that its branches come forth. It is impossible to go to the tree* unless one has these attributes."

This group had a great sense of unity, and did not want some to go to the tree and some to remain behind. They realized that not all would be able to go to the tree, since some had the needed attributes, but others did not. Therefore, all of them remained so as to give the rest an opportunity to strive and gain the attributes necessary to allow them to come to the tree.

They followed this plan, and they struggled and worked until all of them had these attributes. When all of them had the necessary attributes, they all had the same idea, and all of them agreed* on one way as being the true path to the tree.

---

on the face of the earth" (Numbers 12:3). Therefore, he could be the one to receive the Torah (*Likutey Halakhoth, Sefer Torah* 3:5).

All three of these concepts come into play in writing a Torah scroll. The letters themselves represent faith (see *Likutey Moharan* 18). Furthermore, the letters must be perfect, even to the point of a *yod* (*kotzo shel yod*). The *yod* represents humility, because it is the smallest letter in the Hebrew alphabet. Moreover, it represents the World to Come (see *Menachoth* 29b), and the essence of the World to Come is humility (*Likutey Moharan Tinyana* 72).

Finally, the Torah scroll must be written for the sake of God and for the sanctity of the Torah. This represents fear and reverence, as it is written, "You must fear the great and awesome Name" (Deuteronomy 28:58). Thus, by keeping the commandment to write a Torah scroll, one brings the tree to oneself (*Likutey Halakhoth, Sefer Torah* 3:8).

The four concepts of the tree also parallel the four sounds of the shofar: *tekiah* (a long sound), *shevarim* (three short blasts), *teruah* (a stacatto), and the final *tekiah*.

The *tekiah* denotes reverence and fear, as it is written, "Shall the *tekiah* of a shofar be sounded in a city and the people not tremble" (Amos 3:6). *Shevarim* is a "broken sound," and it denotes faith and prayer. *Teruah* denotes humility and prophecy like that of Moses (cf. *Likutey Halakhoth, Choshen Mishpat, Sheluchim* 4:15). The final *tekiah* represents the trunk of the tree, which is truth.

The trunk of the tree includes all the plants in the world. All grow through truth, as it is written, "Truth will grow forth from the earth" (Psalms 85:12; *Likutey Halakhoth, Choshen Mishpat, Sheluchim* 4:16).

go to the tree. Through faith, reverence, and humility, one can attain truth, which is the trunk of the tree. But the concept of truth is that of unity, since "truth is one" (*Likutey Moharan* 51). But since space derives from multiplicity, both of positions and dimensions, the concept of unity is above space. Therefore, when one attains the attribute of truth, one can approach the tree, which is above space (*Chokhmah U'Tevunah* 20:5).

all of them agreed. As long as the groups were far from the tree's attributes, there was no

They set out, and after a while, they were able to see the tree at a distance. However, when they looked at the tree, it was not standing in space.* The tree did not exist in space, and since it did not have a place, it was impossible* to approach it.

I was also with them, and I said, "I can bring you* to the tree. This tree does not have any place at all, since it is above the concept of space.* It is also above the concept of little holding much, since this concept is also an aspect of space. It is obvious that the concept

true peace between them. But when they came close to the concept of the tree, they all agreed (*Likutey Halakhoth*, *Sefer Torah* 3:11). Furthermore since Torah is one, when they all attained truth, they could all be united.

not standing in space. The tree is above space. This is the ultimate level of "little holding much." Since the Torah pertains to this concept, all Israel was able to stand between the poles of the ark, which contained the Torah (see Rashi on Joshua 3:9). In the Temple, also, people stood crowded together, but when they bowed, they had sufficient space (*Avoth* 5:5). In Jerusalem, no one ever said "the place is too crowded" (ibid.). The Land of Israel is called "land of the deer" (Ezekiel 20:6), because it can stretch to hold its populace (*Gittin* 57a). When the Messiah comes, all the Israelites who have ever lived will fit into the Holy Land.

The higher the level of holiness, the less importance space has. The epitome of this was the ark itself, which did not take up any space at all (*Likutey Halakhoth*, *Sefer Torah* 3:6).

The Torah itself is a paradigm of little holding much, since each letter in the Torah supports many universes. The letters of the Torah were used to create many universes. Furthermore, each word of the Torah contains many concepts. Thus, for example, the Hebrew word for man, *adam*, contains the forms and attributes of every human being who would ever exist. (Rabbi Nachman said this explicitly to Rabbi Nathan.)

Thus, when somebody writes a Torah scroll, he is bringing the actual letters, which are above space, into the space of the parchment (*Likutey Halakhoth*, *Sefer Torah* 3:7; also see *Oneg Shabbath*, p. 80).

The Book of Creation (*Sefer Yetzirah* 1:5) speaks of all reality as consisting of five dimensions, the three dimensions of space, time, and the moral, spiritual dimension. The Torah relates to the moral dimension, and hence, is above the dimensions of space.

it was impossible. Literally, "how was it possible to come to it?"

I can bring you. Only a tzaddik who can transcend space can bring people to the tree (*Likutey Etzoth* B, *Tzaddik* 94).

above the concept of space. This tree elevates a person to the Throne of Glory, on the level where God is referred to as *Makom*, meaning "place." God is called this, as the Midrash says, "because He is the 'place' of the world, and the world is not His place" (*Bereshith Rabbah* 68:10). Before the giving of the Torah, God elevated the Israelites to the level of being above space, as He said, "I lifted you on wings of eagles and brought

of little holding much always involves the concept of space, no matter how little space is involved.

"However, the concept of little holding much that I have is at the very end of space,* beyond which there is no space at all. Therefore, I can carry you to the tree, which is totally above space."

you to Me" (Exodus 19:4). The "wings of eagles," are the wings of the divine commandments, alluded to in the verse, "As an eagle stirs up its nest, hovering over its young..." (Deuteronomy 32:11).

Our sages teach that when God said that He brought the Israelites "on wings of eagles," He brought them from Rameses to Sukkoth, a distance of 120 miles, in a single day. He did this by allowing the Israelites to transcend space.

The concept of transcending space is realized through the commandment of *Tzitzith* (tassles, as on the tallith). The Talmud states that the meditation involving *Tzitzith* brings a person up to the Throne of Glory, which is above the concept of space (*Likutey Halakhoth*, *Tzitzith* 3:8).

It is therefore taught that, through *Tzitzith*, the exiles will be gathered. They are now separated by space, because they are in different places. But when they transcend space, they will all be together (*Likutey Halakhoth*, *Tzitzith* 3:9).

This is also related to the concept of sacrifice. An animal does not have "knowledge" (Daath). The concept of "knowledge" is that of joining and unification, as in the verse, "Adam knew Eve his wife" (Genesis 4:1). Therefore, when a person has full knowledge, he is able to transcend space. An animal, however, does not have knowledge, and therefore is bound totally by space.

The Holy Temple, however, was an aspect that transcended space, as discussed earlier. It is thus taught, "Jerusalem is higher that the entire Land of Israel, and the Land of Israel is higher than all other lands" (*Zevachim* 54b). This is derived from the verse, which says of Jerusalem, "You shall go up to the place" (Deuteronomy 17:8). This indicates that Jerusalem is related to God, who is called the Place of the universe. All lands and all places are united in the Temple through the Foundation Stone (*Evven HaShethiyah*).

When animals are sacrificed in the Temple, it is as if the animals are finding their place in the shadow or in the branches of the tree. They are elevated from the arena of space to the arena that is above space. When the person bringing the sacrifice vicariously identifies with the animal, then he, too, transcends space (*Likutey Halakhoth*, *Tzitzith* 3:13).

On Rosh HaShanah, through the sounding of the shofar, we also ascend on the tree to the Throne of Glory, which is above space. Since sin only exists in the realm of space, when we transcend the arena of space, we also transcend the boundaries of sin, and God can judge us for merit. This is also the concept of *teshuvah*–repentance (*Likutey Halakhoth*, *Choshen Mishpat*, *Sheluchim* 4:16).

very end of space. The hunchback therefore existed in space, but just barely. He actually existed on the interface between the realm of space and the realm above space. Thus, he could enter the realm above space and also transport others there.

This is alluded to when Abraham told the angels to rest "under the tree" (Genesis

(The hunchback was on the level of the intermediate concept between space and that which is above space. He possessed the highest possible concept of little holding much, at the end of space, above which the word "place" does not apply at all. Anything higher than this is totally above the concept of space. Therefore, he could carry them from within space to a concept that is above space. Understand this well.)

I took them and carried them to the tree.* Therefore, I have the word of these men that I possess the highest concept of little holding much. (He appeared to be a hunchback because he carried much on his shoulders, being a case of little holding much.)

I am now giving you this as a gift—that you should be like me.

When he finished there was great joy and very great rejoicing.

The Sixth Day*

On the sixth day they were also rejoicing, and they yearned very much, saying, "How could the one without hands be brought here?" Suddenly, he appeared and said, "Here I am! I have come to your wedding!" He spoke to them in the same manner as the other beggars, and kissed them.

Then he said: You think there is something wrong with my hands.

18:4), rather than inviting them into his house. He wanted to bring them under the Tree of Life, above the concept of space.

This is alluded to in the expression "under the tree." In the Hebrew "the tree" is ha-etz. Since vav follows heh, peh follows eyin, and kof follows tzadi, the letters "under ha-etz" are vav peh kof, which have a numerical value of 186. This is the same numerical value as the word makom, meaning place. This indicates that the tree is "above" the concept of place (Oneg Shabbath, p. 80).

carried them to the tree. The tzaddik who transcends space can overcome the limitations of space and unite all peoples. He can bring them to the ultimate peace (Likutey Halakhoth, Sefer Torah 3:11). This is the concept of the Messiah, who will bring peace to all the world. This is why the couple said that there would be great joy if the hunchback was there. Furthermore, he could bring people to the tree, which was the source of great joy and delight, as we see in the story.

The Sixth Day. Rabbi Nachman completed the story of the sixth day on the next Tuesday (April 10) (Sichoth HaRan 149). It was shortly before Passover, and his house was being replastered for the festival. He had gone to Rabbi Aaron, the official rabbi of Breslov, and a group was around him. When they told him an anecdote, he said that it was related to the story of the sixth day, and he immediately told it (Sichoth HaRan 151).

Actually, there is nothing wrong with my hands. I have great power in my hands.* But I do not use the power in my hands in this physical world, since I need this power for something else entirely. Regarding this, I have the word of the Water Castle.*

Once, a number of men were sitting together and each one boasted about the power in his hands.* One boasted that he had a certain power in his hands, and another boasted that he had a different power. Finally, one boasted that the power in his hands was such that if an arrow* were shot he could retrieve it.* He had such great power in his hands that even after an arrow had been shot, he could return it and bring it back to him.

---

hands. Although this beggar appears not to have any hands, he actually has tremendous powers in his hands. It is just that his hands are above the physical plane and therefore cannot be seen (*Likutey Etzoth B, Tzaddik* 96).

Water Castle. *Vassiriken schloss* in Yiddish.

power in his hands. There are four powers discussed here: the power to retrieve an arrow, giving by receiving, conferring wisdom, and holding back the wind. These are discussed individually.

arrow. In one sense, shooting an arrow refers to sexual misdeeds. It is thus taught that the sperm "shoots like an arrow" (*Yebamoth* 65a). A sexual misdeed is like an arrow shot at the Shekhinah, which is the paradigmatic Feminine Principle. A tzaddik can undo the damage done by sexual misdeeds and hence "retrieve" the arrow (*Likutey Halakhoth, Evven HaEzer, P'ru U'R'vu* 3:10).

retrieve it. This is an attribute of God, as He said, "My hand will grasp judgment ... I will make My arrows drunk with blood" (Deuteronomy 32:41,42). "Grasping judgment" denotes grasping the instrument of judgment and retrieving it. Rashi thus says that this means that God can shoot an arrow and then make it come back (end of story). In this context, the arrow denotes divine punishment.

Rabbi Nathan likens God's shooting arrows to giving the Holy Land to the seven Canaanite nations. He then retrieves the arrows by taking the land from these nations and giving it to Israel (*Likutey Halakhoth, Pesach, Roshay Perakim* 9:3).

One may raise a general objection here. Why does the story say that he has the power to *shoot* the arrow and then retrieve it? Why does it mention shooting? Would it not be better not to shoot the arrow in the first place?

But actually, shooting the arrow is in itself part of the healing process. If the tzaddik can shoot the arrow, then he can undo the spiritual damage at its very root. The tzaddik does this by identifying with the evil deed, and thus "shooting the arrow."

A good example of this is bringing a sacrifice, which is meant to rectify the world of Asiyah. The slaughter-knife comes from the same root as the arrows (cf. Proverbs 25:18)

I challenged him, "What kind of arrow can you retrieve? There are ten types of arrows.* This is because there are ten types of poisons.* When a person shoots an arrow, he first coats it with some type of poison. There are ten types of poison. When one coats the arrow with the first type of poison, it does a certain degree of harm. If the arrow is coated with the second type of poison, it does worse harm. Thus, there are ten types of poison, each one more harmful than the other.

"That is why there are ten types of arrows. All the arrows are actually the same, but since there are different poisons with which the arrows are rubbed, and there are ten types of poison, it is considered as if there are ten types of arrows."

and are the instruments of Esau, as Isaac blessed him, "By your sword you shall live" (Genesis 27:40). The name *Esau* comes from the root *asah*, which is the same as the root of Asiyah; Esau is the evil aspect of Asiyah. By applying the knife to the animal, however, one rectifies the evil of Esau at its very root. This is also the reason that we recite the sacrificial readings as the first part of the morning service. This portion of the service corresponds to Asiyah (*Likutey Halakhoth, Tolaim* 4:7).

It is taught that a person should draw people close with his right hand and repulse them with his left (*Sotah* 47a). This is also the concept of shooting an arrow and bringing it back.

ten types of arrows. The ten types of arrows denote ten types of spiritual damage caused by sin. It is thus written, "Your arrows have gone deep into me, and Your hand has come down upon me" (Psalms 38:3). These arrows of sin caused the exile of Israel, as it is written that the Israelites said to God, "You made me a target for the arrow" (Lamentations 3:12) (*Likutey Halakhoth, Rosh HaShanah* 6:12; for other references to arrows, see *Likutey Halakhoth, Pesach, Roshay Perakim* 6:5, 9:4).

As we shall see, water is associated with the power of healing. The arrows, on the other hand, are associated with the element of dust. The closer something is to the earth, the greater the power of evil (*Likutey Halakhoth, Tolaim* 4:6).

The arrows denote the powers of evil, which come from the Breaking of the Vessels. This is associated with the expansion of the Tetragrammaton, which adds up to 52, known as *BaN*. As we shall see, this expansion parallels the element of dust (*Likutey Halakhoth, Tolaim* 4:8). The ten arrows then allude to the ten sefiroth of *BaN*.

The ten arrows can also allude to the ten nations that originally occupied the Holy Land (mentioned in Genesis 15:18–21). The *Targum* thus renders the verse, "he crushed their arrows" (Numbers 24:8), as "he vacated their land" (*Zimrath HaAretz*).

poisons. The *Zohar* speaks of ten unclean Crowns (*Tikkuney Zohar* 69, 108b). "Crown" is the highest of the sefiroth, and the ten unclean Crowns are the root forces of all evil. The ten poisons in the story denote these Crowns (*Likutey Halakhoth, Tolaim* 4:2).

The poisons represent the different ways that a person can defile the covenant of Abraham through sexual misdeeds (*Likutey Halakhoth, P'ru U'R'vu* 3:10).

I therefore asked him, "What kind of arrow* can you bring back?" I also asked him if he could retrieve the arrow only before it hit its victim, or if he could bring it back even after it hit.

What kind of arrow. The remedy for the arrows is through repentance. This parallels the verse, "In the beginning God created the heaven and earth" (Genesis 1:1), which the Talmud speaks of as being the first of the Ten Sayings of Creation (*Rosh HaShanah* 32a). Since the verse does not say that God said anything, this is a "hidden saying." As a hidden saying, it includes all ten (cf. *Likutey Moharan Tinyana* 12). This parallels the sefirah of Kether, which is the highest sefirah, and includes all ten sefiroth (*Likutey Halakhoth, Rosh HaShanah* 6:12).

Since the first verse of the Torah includes all sayings, it also includes evil. The Torah therefore continues "The earth was desolate and void" (Genesis 1:2). But the verse then continues, "The spirit of God hovered over the face of the water." The Midrash states that this is the "spirit of the Messiah" (cf. Isaiah 11:2). The Messiah works with water, which denotes repentance, as it is written, "Pour out your heart like water" (Lamentations 2:19) (*Likutey Halakhoth, Rosh HaShanah* 6:3).

Thus, Kether includes everything, even evil. Since it can include evil, it can also rectify evil, and therefore, it is the root of repentance. This beggar had the powers of Kether, just as the Messiah will, to rectify all ten levels of evil. Since Kether contains all ten levels of holiness, it can rectify all ten levels of evil (*Likutey Halakhoth, Rosh HaShanah* 6:7).

The first saying of creation is hidden; thus, it represents God's hidden power, which also sustains evil. Therefore, this hidden saying is also the source of all ten arrows. These arrows are shot at the Princess, who represents the souls of Israel. The arrows come from the realm of the unclean.

The one who heals the Princess has the power both to shoot the arrows and to retrieve them. This is the power of the hidden saying.

This also answers the question, "If he can remove the arrows, why does he shoot them in the first place? Would it not be better not to shoot them at all?"

But he "shoots the arrows and retrieves them" because he is associated with the hidden saying, which is the source of both evil and its rectification. The arrows are needed so that free will and free choice exist in the world. But once evil exists, and the arrows have been shot, there must also be the means of retrieving and removing them.

This beggar has no hands precisely because he is associated with the hidden saying. Just as God's power is not detectable in this saying, so the beggar's hands are not detectable. Nevertheless, they have the greatest power of them all (*Likutey Halakhoth, Rosh HaShanah* 6:12).

The first word of this hidden saying is *Bereshith*. The *Tikkuney Zohar* states that this has the same letters as *yira bosheth*, which means "fear, shame." This is the concept of repentance, whose main ingredients are fear of God and shame for one's sins (see *Likutey Moharan Tinyana* 72). Therefore, the first word, *Bereshith*, includes the concept of repentance, which removes the arrows.

God therefore gave us ten days of repentance between Rosh HaShanah and Yom Kippur. The ten days of repentance serve to remove the ten arrows through our repentance. The

To the second question, he replied, "I can retrieve an arrow even after it hits* its target." However to the first question he said that he could only retrieve one type of arrow.

I said to him, "If this is true, then you cannot heal the Queen's Daughter.* If you can only turn back one type of arrow,* you cannot heal her."

arrows are the blemish that we make in the Shekhinah through our sins (*Likutey Halakhoth, Rosh HaShanah* 6:13; cf. 6:4; also see Ibid., *Roshay Perakim* 6:7).

On Yom Kippur we recite the confession ten times. This also serves to remove the ten arrows. The arrows have injured the Shekhinah, but with our confessions, we are able to remove them.

While reciting the confession (*viduy*), it is a custom to strike the heart with the fist. This alludes to the fact that the arrows are removed through the power of the hands. Closely related to this is the custom of lifting one's hands to God when praying for forgiveness (*Likutey Halakhoth, Rosh HaShanah, Roshay Perakim* 6:9).

Our sages teach that, "It was not necessary to begin the Torah with *Bereshith*" (cf. Rashi on Genesis 1:1). But it was done "to show the strength of His deeds" (Psalms 111:6). This is the strength of God's "hand," which is contained in *Bereshith*, alluded to by the handless beggar. This, as Rashi explained, was to remove the ten nations, who occupied the land previously (see Genesis 15:18–21). These ten nations, as we have seen, parallel the ten arrows (*Likutey Halakhoth, Pesach, Roshay Perakim* 9:3).

As we have seen, the concept of slaughtering a sacrifice rectifies the effects of the ten arrows. The ritual slaughter involves a back and forth movement of the knife. This back and forth movement is also related to the concept of shooting and retrieving.

Rabbi Nachman also speaks of praying with the Attribute of Justice. This takes the arrow, which is the means of punishment, and uses it as a means of healing. Prayer is also called an arrow. Jacob thus said that he captured the land of the Amorites with his "sword and bow," and the "bow" is interpreted to mean prayer (*Likutey Halakhoth, Tolaim* 4:7).

In general, there are four aspects of ten here; ten arrows, ten walls, ten types of pulse, and ten types of song. We shall discuss their relationship shortly (*Likutey Halakhoth, Pesach, Roshay Perakim* (9).

after it hits. It would seem to be a difficult enough task to retrieve an arrow after it was fired. But to retrieve an arrow and undo its effects after it has hit its target is truly remarkable. This is obviously to be interpreted on a spiritual level rather than on a physical plane (*Likutey Halakhoth, Evven HaEzer* 3:10).

Queen's Daughter. The Divine Presence (Shekhinah), which is identified with the souls of Israel. See story "The Lost Princess" (in *The Lost Princess*).

one type of arrow. We thus see that some tzaddikim can rectify some evil, but it takes an extraordinary tzaddik to be able to rectify all types of evil (*Rimzey Maasioth*). Elsewhere, Rabbi Nachman writes that in order to take a *pidyon* (redemption) a tzaddik must know

One of the men present boasted that he had such power in his hands that whenever he took or received something from another, he was actually giving to him.* For him the very act of receiving was an act of giving. Therefore, he was a master of charity.*

I asked him what type of charity he gave, since there are ten types of charity. He replied that he gave a tithe.*

I said to him, "If this is so, you cannot heal the Queen's Daughter. You cannot even approach the place where she is; you can only go through one wall* in the place where she is staying. You cannot get to where she is."

how to plead before all twenty-four heavenly courts (*Sichoth HaRan* 175; *Likutey Moharan* 215).

actually giving to him. The Talmud thus says that when a person gives a gift to a very important person, the acceptance of the gift is in itself a gift. Thus, when a woman gives an important man a gift, it is counted as if he had given her something of monetary value (Kiddushin 7a).

Rabbi Nachman also once said, "When I take money from someone, I am actually giving him something. My taking is actually giving" (*Sichoth HaRan* 150). This is the ultimate level of the tzaddik (*Likutey Etzoth B, Tzaddik* 96).

charity. Every time he accepts something, he is actually giving. Since there is no limit to how much he can accept, his "giving" is limitless.

However, this is also the concept of charity. When a person gives charity, the spiritual benefits that he receives are much greater than any amount that he gives.

This concept of charity is most important, since the entire world was created for the sake of charity. Moreover, the very creation of the world was an act of altruism and charity on the part of God. It is thus written, "I have said, the world is built on charity" (Psalms 89:3). Furthermore, the paradigm of charity was Abraham, and it is thus taught that the world was created for the sake of Abraham (*Likutey Halakhoth*, Pesach, *Roshay Perakim* 9:4).

As we see in the story, the walls of water stand through charity. This charity is the logic of the Vacated Space that God will reveal in the Ultimate Future (see *Likutey Moharan* 64; *Likutey Halakhoth, Tolaim* 4:10).

tithe. *Ma'aser*. That is, one tenth of his income. This is the concept of "tithe of money" (*ma'aser kesafim*), which is discussed in Jewish law.

one wall. That is, through one of the ten walls of water surrounding the Water Castle, as we see later in the story. These walls consist of waves in the water, as the story later states explicitly.

Charity is associated with water, as it is written, "Your charity is like the waves of the sea" (Isaiah 48:18) (end of story). Rabbi Nachman also taught explicitly that charity is water (*Likutey Moharan Tinyana* 15; *Likutey Halakhoth, Rosh HaShanah* 6:8). Charity is related to the sefirah of Chesed, which is also associated with water.

One of the men present boasted about the power in his hands, saying that there were officials in the world. These are highly placed people who are in charge of cities and nations.* Each one needs wisdom. Through his hands he could give them wisdom.* He did this by laying hands on them.

I asked him, "What type of wisdom can you confer with your hands? There are ten types of wisdom."

When he replied what kind of wisdom, I said to him, "If this is the case, you cannot heal the Queen's Daughter. You cannot understand her pulse, since there are ten types of pulse.* You can only con-

Therefore, one can only enter the walls of water through charity. If one can grant all ten types of charity, one can enter through all ten walls leading to the Water Castle (*Likutey Halakhoth, Rosh HaShanah* 6:8).

Both charity and the entire Torah are likened to water. It is for this reason that charity includes all of the Torah. The Torah itself is referred to as charity, as it is written, "It will be charity for us if we keep all this Torah" (Deuteronomy 6:25). Charity, however, is given only through the tzaddik, as it is written, "The tzaddik has mercy and gives" (Psalms 37:21).

Since the environment of the tzaddik is charity (*tzedakah*), which is likened to water, the tzaddik is likened to a fish. It is therefore said of the children of Joseph (the paradigm of the tzaddik and personification of Yesod), "They shall increase like fish..." (Genesis 48:16). When a tzaddik takes charity, he is able to grow spiritually, through his worship and study of the Torah. This is great merit for the one who gives him charity. Thus, whenever the tzaddik takes, he gives, as we saw earlier.

Since fish represent the tzaddik, who is completely holy, everything in a fish is kosher. With mammals and birds, some parts of their bodies are not kosher, such as forbidden fats, the sciatic nerve (*gid ha-nasheh*), and the blood. In the case of a kosher fish, on the other hand, everything is kosher.

This is also the reason that a fish does not require any kind of ritual slaughter. Other animals need this rectification, but fish are inherently holy, just like a tzaddik (*Likutey Halakhoth, Yoreh Deah, Dagim* 4:1).

These are ... This appears only in the Yiddish.

give them wisdom. Laying of hands confers wisdom. Thus, Moses laid his hands on Joshua to give him wisdom. The Torah says, "Joshua, son of Nun, was full of the spirit of wisdom, because Moses had laid his hands upon him" (Deuteronomy 34:9). Joshua thus became a man "who has wind-spirit in him" (Numbers 27:18). This meant that he knew how to determine each person's wind-spirit (*ruach*), which is manifested in that person's pulse (*Likutey Halakhoth, Tolaim* 4:2).

ten types of pulse. This is discussed at length in the Zoharic literature (*Tikkuney Zohar* 70, p. 108a; see *Shaar Ruach HaKodesh*, p. 14). These ten types of pulse beats correspond

fer one type of wisdom, and therefore only understand one type of pulse."

One of the men present boasted that he had such great power in his hands that when there was a storm, he could hold it back* with his hands. Then with his hands he could make the wind blow with the proper force* so that the wind was beneficial.

I asked him, "What kind of wind can you hold with your hands? There are ten kinds of winds." He described the type of wind that he could hold, and I said, "If that is the case, you cannot heal the Queen's Daughter. You can only play one type of melody. She can only be

---

to the ten Hebrew vowel points. The pulse beat is related to the shape of the vowel point.

In Hebrew, the word for pulse is *defek*, from the word *dafak*, meaning to knock (as on a door). This is alluded to in the verse, "The sound of my beloved knocks..." (Song of Songs 5:2) (*Likutey Halakhoth, Rosh HaShanah, Roshay Perakim* 6:2).

The ten types of pulse relate to the vowel points, which are associated with the universe of Beriyah (*Likutey Halakhoth*, Pesach, *Roshay Perakim* 9:3).

Human life depends on the pulse. The ten pulse types parallel the ten types of song (see *Likutey Moharan Tinyana* 24). Therefore, healing requires knowing the pulses, and then knowing what song to use as a remedy (*Likutey Halakhoth, P'ru U'R'vu* 3:1).

hold it back. This is alluded to in the verse, "Who gathers up the wind in His palm" (Proverbs 30:4). Rabbi Nachman taught that this was related to the concept of melody, as we see in the story (end of story).

The wind relates to air, the highest of the four elements. This relates to the expansion of the Tetragrammaton that adds up to 72, known as *AB*, the highest of the four expansions. It is on the level of Chokhmah and Atziluth. This is also the level of the cantillations, which are an aspect of song. (This is discussed at greater length below.)

The concept of song comes from the wind and breath in the lungs. The Talmud also notes that a north wind blew on David's lyre (Aolean harp), and caused it to play music (*Berakhoth* 3b; *Likutey Halakhoth*, Pesach, *Roshay Perakim* 9:3).

Holding the wind is an attribute of God, as it is written, "The storm wind does His bidding" (Psalms 148:8) (*Likutey Halakhoth*, Pesach, *Roshay Perakim* 9:3).

proper force. *Mishkal* in Hebrew, which denotes balance. The Yiddish says, "With the hand, He can make the wind with a measure, so that there should be a wind as we need it, and the proper measure."

healed through melody,* and there are ten types of melody.* But you can only play one type of melody, out of these ten."

healed through melody. From this we see, in general, the importance of song and melody. The tzaddik must know all ten categories of song, because the Princess can only be healed through song and joy (*Sichoth HaRan* 273).

This healing takes place in the Water Castle. Joy and song, however, are associated with water, as it is written, "You shall draw water with joy from the well of salvation" (Isaiah 12:3). Therefore, when water was drawn for the special Sukkoth libations, it was a special time of rejoicing, known as *Simchath Beth HaSho'evah*. On the seventh day, people would take the willow (*hoshanah*), which also grew by water, since the Torah describes it as "willow of the brook" (Leviticus 23:40) (*Likutey Halakhoth, Rosh HaShanah, Roshay Perakim* 6:2).

This is also the concept of Purim, which is a festival of joy. Passover is the first of the three festivals, but preparations for it are made on Purim, which occurs a month earlier (see *Megillah* 32a; *Orach Chaim* 427). Mordechai is the tzaddik who can heal even those who are very ill spiritually, and he does it through joy and song. He heals the Princess, who denotes the souls of Israel (*Likutey Halakhoth*, Basar BeChalav 5:19).

Both song and the pulse depend on wind and breath. Therefore the energy of song gives strength to the energy of the pulse. The wind associated with music and the pulse also upholds the walls of water. The Princess also escapes the arrows by running into these walls of water. Therefore, all four concepts in this story are interdependent, and hence all four major powers are in the hands. These correspond to the four concepts of written Hebrew: cantillations (*taamim*), vowel points (*nekudoth*), crowns (*tagim*), and letters (*othioth*), referred to collectively as *TaNTA*. All of these are interdependent. Everything, however, ultimately depends on melody, which corresponds to the cantillations, and hence is the highest level of the four (*Likutey Halakhoth, Tolaim* 4:11).

ten types of melody. Rabbi Nachman himself taught that the Ten Psalms were a "general rectification" (*tikkun kellali*) for all sins, particularly sexual sins, and especially those involving emitting semen in vain (*Likutey Moharan* 205; *Likutey Moharan Tinyana* 92; see end of story). These involved the ten types of melody found in the psalms. The Ten Psalms are numbers 16, 32, 41, 42, 59, 77, 90, 105, 137, 150.

It is highly significant that the Ten Psalms were revealed during the week before Rabbi Nachman began to tell the story of the Seven Beggars (*Alim Leterufah*, letter of Tulchin at end of book; cf. *Sichoth HaRan* 141, *Parparoth LeChokhmah* on *Likutey Moharan Tinyana* 75). It is significant that the concept of the Ten Psalms is also related to the power of charity mentioned here in the story, since Rabbi Nachman said, "If someone comes to my grave, gives a penny to charity, and recites these Ten Psalms, I will yank him out of Gehenom by his *peyoth* [earlocks]" (*Chayay Moharan* 45a 41; cf. *Nevey Tzaddikim*, p. 66).

It is also significant to note that this relates to the sixth day. The sixth day parallels the sefirah of Yesod, which pertains to the sexual organ. Hence, the rectification for sexual misdeeds is part of this day's story.

The sixth day was also the day when man committed the first sin. This was the shooting of the ten arrows. The rectification must go to the root of the evil, and therefore takes place also on the sixth day.

The psalms as a whole also contain all ten different types of song (*Tikkuney Zohar* 13; *Likutey Moharan Tinyana* 92). King David ended the book with Psalm 150, which contains the expression *halelu-hu* ("praise Him") ten times. The last of these is, "Praise Him with cymbals of *teruah*" (Psalms 150:5), because the *teruah* (stacatto) also includes all ten types of song (*Likutey Halakhoth, Evven HaEzer, P'ru U'R'vu* 3:10).

Through the ten types of song, we can balance the ten types of wind. The ten winds, however, form the ten types of waves, which are the ten walls around the Water Castle. Therefore, when one knows the ten songs, one can penetrate the ten walls (*Likutey Halakhoth, Rosh HaShanah, Roshay Perakim* 6:3).

Sin and spiritual damage are associated with sadness and depression. The healing is therefore through song, which brings joy. With his hands this beggar could enter the nine chambers of joy (cf. *Likutey Moharan* 24; *Likutey Halakhoth, Orach Chaim, Hodaah* 6:20; cf. *Likutey Halakhoth, Evven HaEzer, P'ru U'R'vu* 3:1).

The "hidden saying," *Bereshith*, also contains all ten types of songs. It is therefore taught that *Bereshith* has the letters *shir taev* (*Tikkuney Zohar* 10; *Likutey Halakhoth, Rosh HaShanah* 6:14).

The sacrifice and libation offerings were meant to refine fallen souls and raise the sparks of the souls that had fallen deep into the realm of evil. While the libation offerings (*nesakhim*) were being poured, the Levites would sing. This was because the healing of the Princess was through song (*Likutey Halakhoth, Rosh HaShanah* 6:14).

The ten songs were also alluded to in the ten sounds of the shofar. On Rosh HaShanah the shofar is sounded in the following manner:

tekiah shevarim teruah tekiah

tekiah shevarim tekiah

tekiah teruah tekiah

Thus, there are a total of ten sounds. These allude to the ten types of song.

Furthermore, on Rosh HaShanah, in the mussaf service, ten verses of *malkhiyoth* (kingship), ten verses of *zikhronoth* (remembrances), and ten verses of *shofroth* (shofar sounds) are said. Each set of ten verses also parallels the ten types of song.

Rosh HaShanah is the beginning of the ten days of repentance; therefore it has these ten types of song. Song is the basis of repentance, since song leads to joy, and joy brings one to the side of merit (*Likutey Moharan* 282). It is only through the ten types of song that those who are far from God can be brought back (*Likutey Halakhoth, P'ru U'R'vu* 3:10).

The ten days of repentance also parallel the ten types of song. We begin these ten days with Rosh HaShanah, where all ten types of song are brought into play through the ten sounds of the shofar. Shofar is the rectification of these ten types of song, as it is written, "Make song good with the *teruah* sound" (Psalms 33:3). The psalm says, "God will rise in *teruah*, God in the sound of the shofar. Sing to God sing..." (Psalms 47:6). This indicates that after sounding the shofar, one can sing all types of songs properly (*Likutey Halakhoth, P'ru U'R'vu* 3:10).

All the people there spoke up and asked me, "What is your ability?"

I replied, "I can do what you cannot do. In each of the cases that you discussed there are nine portions that you cannot accomplish. I can accomplish them all."*

The ten days of repentance end with Yom Kippur. This completes the ten types of song (*Likutey Halakhoth, P'ru U'R'vu* 3:11).

I can accomplish them all. The handless beggar thus had four powers: (1) to remove the arrows; (2) the power of charity, to go through the ten walls; (3) the power to confer wisdom and know the pulse; and (4) the power to control the wind and play all types of music.

On Sukkoth, we take the four species in hand to strengthen the hands of this beggar. Then on Simchath Torah we perfect the concept of joy and song when we complete the Torah and begin it once again. We begin the Torah with the word *Bereshith*, which is the hidden saying (*Likutey Halakhoth, Rosh HaShanah, Roshay Perakim* 6:2).

The four species are the palm (*lulav*), willow (*aravah*), myrtle (*hadas*), and citron (*ethrog*) (Leviticus 23:40). The *lulav* has the form of an arrow, and this strengthens the power to remove the arrows. The "willows of the brook" strengthen the power of the handless beggar to penetrate the walls of water. The myrtle parallels the life of the soul in Chokhmah (Wisdom), and this gives the power to understand the ten pulsebeats. Finally, the *ethrog* perfects the concept of joy and song.

The Torah is then completed on Simchath Torah, with the verse, "...and all the mighty *hand* ... which Moses wrought in the sight of all Israel" (Deuteronomy 34:12). This strengthens the concept of the hand. We then immediately begin the Torah with *Bereshith*, the "hidden saying" (*Likutey Halakhoth, Rosh HaShanah, Roshay Perakim* 6:5).

There are four groups of ten in this story: ten arrows, ten walls (charity), ten types of pulse (wisdom in hand), and ten songs (power to hold back wind). All are ten.

These four parallel the four supernal universes, Atziluth (Nearness), Beriyah (Creation), Yetzirah (Formation), and Asiyah (Making). These parallel the four letters in the Tetragrammaton (YHVH).

They also parallel the four expansions of the Tetragrammaton. They are:

YOD HY VYV HY 72 AB

YOD HY VAV HY 63 SaG

YOD HA VAV HA 45 MaH

YOD HH VV HH 52 BaN

They also parallel the four concepts involved in writing, referred to as *TaNTA: taamim* (cantillations), *nekudoth* (vowel points), *tagim* (crowns), and *othioth* (letters).

In addition to this, they parallel the four elements: fire, air, water, and dust.

They also parallel the four levels of creation: the inert, plants, animals, and humans (speaking creatures).

The final parallel is the four parts of the daily morning service, the *Korbanoth* (the sacrificial readings), *Pesukey deZimra* (the Introductory Psalms), the Sh'ma and its blessings, and the Amidah.

All these groups contain four elements, and they parallel the four elements in this story.

The four expansions of the Tetragrammaton relate to the highest levels of creation, known as Adam Kadmon. AB is above all comprehension, and nothing can be said about it at all. SaG was the beginning of all revelation, from which the Universe of Nekudim (points) came into existence. These points were the original vessels. BaN represents the breaking of the vessels. Finally, the Broken Vessels were rectified when MaH and BaN were unified. This parallels the unification in Atziluth, which is lower than Adam Kadmon, of Zer Anpin and Malkhuth.

The Princess denotes Malkhuth, which is God's kingdom. The main purpose of creation was to reveal Malkhuth. God therefore brought forth the original Vessels, which were known as the Kings (from Genesis 36:31–39). As a result of the imperfections built in creation, these Vessels were broken. This was to bring the concept of evil and free will into the world. The Breaking of the Vessels created the forces of the Other Side, represented in the story by the king who tried to capture the Princess. This king is the counterpart on the Other Side, of Malkhuth, the Kingdom of God. This evil king wants to capture the Princess, denoting the inner holiness of all things, this being the mystery of the verse, "All glorious, is the Princess inside" (Psalms 45:14).

The Princess is thus in each of the seven Kings of Edom (Genesis 36:31–39), who represent the vessels that were shattered. When the vessels were shattered, and the kings died, the Princess was captured by the evil king. The Princess represents the sparks of holiness that fell down into the realm of the evil husks (*klipoth*), from which the Kings of Edom draw their power.

The Princess can only escape when she goes through the walls of water. This is the rectification, involving the light of MaH. Water is the third element, just as MaH is the third expansion of the Tetragrammaton. It is also for this reason that water cleanses all impurities (*Likutey Halakhoth*, Pesach, *Roshay Perakim* 9:1).

The ten arrows parallel the Universe of Asiyah, the lowest of the four universes. This is the universe where the powers of evil have their strongest hold. It also parallels the element of dust and BaN.

The ten walls of water parallel the Universe of Yetzirah. It also parallels the expansion known as MaH, and the element of water. Thus, Rabbi Akiba told the four who entered *Pardes* that when they ascend they should not say "water water" (*Chagigah* 14b). Yetzirah is the domain of "water," but it is not physical water.

The ten pulses parallel the Universe of Beriyah. This relates to the *nekudoth* (vowel points), which are the second highest level. It also parallels the expansion SaG.

Finally, the ten types of song parallel the Universe of Atziluth. This parallels the *taamim* (cantillations), which are the highest level of expression. Cantillation and song involve the same concept. This is related to the expansion AB (*Likutey Halakhoth*, Tolaim 4:5).

The four powers of the hands are alluded to in the four times that hands are mentioned in the poem "A Woman of Valor" (Proverbs 31:19, 20) (*Chokhmah U'Tevunah* 21:5).

This is the story:
Once there was a king* who desired a Queen's Daughter.* He made all kinds of plots to capture her until he was finally successful and took her captive.*
Then the king had a dream. The Queen's Daughter was standing over him, and she killed him.*

king. The king is a manifestation of the Evil Urge (*Yetzer Hara*), who is known as an "old and foolish king" (Ecclesiastes 4:13) (*Likutey Moharan* 1; *Likutey Halakhoth, Tolaim* 4:2).

As is known, evil came into existence basically with the Breaking of the Vessels. The Vessels are represented by the "Kings of Edom" (Genesis 36:31–39). Therefore, the power of evil that came into existence when the vessels broke is appropriately represented by a king (*Likutey Halakhoth,* Pesach, *Roshay Perakim* 9:1; *Tolaim* 4:3).

This evil king was personified by Pharaoh, who tried to keep the Israelites captive (*Likutey Halakhoth, Tolaim* 4:4).

Queen's Daughter. This is the same as the Princess described in "The Lost Princess" and "The King and the Emperor" (see *The Lost Princess*). See Introduction.

In general, this Princess represents every Jewish soul, which is attacked by the forces of evil (*Sichoth HaRan* 273; *Likutey Halakhoth,* Basar BeChalav 5:19).

In more general terms, the Queen's Daughter is the Shekhinah, which is referred to as the Congregation of Israel (Knesseth Yisroel) (*Likutey Halakhoth,* Rosh HaShanah 6:12; Ibid. *Roshay Perakim* 6:7; *P'ru U'R'vu* 3:10). This is the sefirah of Malkhuth (kingship, royalty), the Kingdom of God (*Likutey Halakhoth,* Pesach, *Roshay Perakim* 9:1). This is the root of all souls and the root of all worlds, since all were created to reveal God's Kingdom (*Likutey Halakhoth, Tolaim* 4:3).

This concept of the Princess is personified in many ways. In one sense it is personified by the entire nation of Israel. It was personified by Pharaoh's daughter, a holy person, whose holiness had been captured by an evil king, her father. Just like the Princess in the story, she tried to rid herself of the king's influence by going to bathe in the water (Exodus 2:5) (*Likutey Halakhoth,* Pesach, *Roshay Perakim* 9:3).

took her captive. The Evil King represents the broken pieces of the shattered vessels. These are the forces of evil that are nourished by the 288 sparks of holiness, which represent the Princess in their power (see "The Lost Princess" in *The Lost Princess*). This is alluded to in the verse, "The earth was desolate and void, with darkness on the deep" (Genesis 1:2) (*Likutey Halakhoth, Tolaim* 4:3).

The capture of the Princess was reenacted on a physical plane when Sarah was taken captive in Pharaoh's palace (Genesis 12:15), and later, when she was taken to Abimelekh's house harem (Genesis 20:2). It was manifested when the Israelites were enslaved in Egypt (*Likutey Halakhoth, Tolaim* 4:4).

killed him. The Evil One realizes that, in the end, evil will be destroyed by the souls of Israel. God thus said, "I will remove the unclean spirit from the world" (Zechariah 13:2). It is

When he woke up, he took this dream to heart. He summoned all the dream interpreters, and they all said that it would come true in its literal meaning, that she would kill him.

The king could not decide what to do with her. If he killed her, it would grieve him. If he sent her away, this would anger him, since another man would then have her. This would frustrate him very much, since he had worked so hard to get her, only to have her belong to another man. Furthermore, if he exiled her and she ended up with another man, there would be all the more chance of the dream coming true. With an ally, it would be even easier for her to kill him.

Still, he was afraid because of the dream, and did not want to keep her near him. Therefore, the king did not know what to do* with her.

As a result of the dream, his love for her gradually began to wane. As time passed, his desire for her grew less and less. The same was true of her. Her love for him declined* more and more until she hated him.* Eventually, she fled.*

thus taught that in the ultimate future, the Evil Urge will be slaughtered (*Sukkah* 52a). This is also the concept of the thanksgiving offering, which involves destroying the evil within the individual bringing it (*Sanhedrin* 43b; *Likutey Halakhoth, Tolaim* 4:2).

Thus, the Kingdom of Evil sees that it will be cast off and destroyed in the end. This was manifested on the physical plane when "God made great plagues for Pharaoh because of Sarai" (Genesis 12:17). Similarly, God came to Abimelekh in a dream (just as the king saw a dream) and told him, "You will die because of the woman you took" (Genesis 20:7) (*Likutey Halakhoth, Tolaim* 4:4).

did not know what to do. The *Yetzer Hara* (Evil Urge) thinks of ways to destroy the soul, even when the soul is in its power (*Likutey Halakhoth, Tolaim* 4:2).

Her love for him declined. At first there was some love between the soul and the Evil Urge. As a result of her exile, she forgot her lofty status and felt some love and closeness to the Evil One. But when she began to realize that he no longer loved her, her love for him also grew weaker (*Likutey Halakhoth, Tolaim* 4:2).

she hated him. The soul also begins to realize that the Evil One wants to destroy her. She therefore begins to hate him and plans how to escape (*Likutey Halakhoth, Tolaim* 4:2).

fled. This had its parallel on the physical plane when Jacob fled from Laban (Genesis 31:20–21). Jacob contained all the souls of Israel and was fleeing from Evil, which was personified by Laban.

It was repeated when the Israelites fled from Pharaoh. It is thus written, "Pharaoh heard that the people had fled" (Exodus 14:5).

King David, also, said, "If I only had the wings of a dove, I would fly away and be at

The king sent* his men to search for her. When they returned, they reported that she was near* the Water Castle.*

rest ... I would rush myself to a shelter from the stormy wind and tempest" (Psalms 55:7, 9) (*Likutey Halakhoth, Tolaim* 4:2).

The king sent. Evil wishes to recapture the internal holiness in all things (*Likutey Halakhoth, Pesach, Roshay Perakim* 9:1). This was expressed on the physical plane when the Egyptians wanted to place the Israelites under their dominion, and said, "Let us deal wisely with them ... lest they increase, and when there is a war, fight against us, and go forth from the land" (Exodus 1:10) (*Likutey Halakhoth, Tolaim* 4:4).

she was near... As on the physical plane, it was reported to Pharaoh that the Israelites had fled and were on the shore of the Red Sea (Exodus 14:5) (*Likutey Halakhoth, Tolaim* 4:4).

Water Castle. When the Princess wanted to escape the king, she went to water, since water cleanses all things. This is why an important step toward purification and repentance is immersion in a mikvah.

Rashi notes that water was created before heaven and earth, and for this reason, the creation of water is not mentioned explicitly in the Torah (Rashi on Genesis 1:1). This is because the creation of water is included in the word *Bereshith* ("In the beginning"), which is the "hidden saying." Water is thus the root of all creation, but the creation of water is concealed in the word *Bereshith*.

As we have seen, *Bereshith* includes the creation of all things, even evil. Therefore, since water comes from this saying, water has an affinity for evil and becomes unclean very easily. Thus, even though a "second level defilement" (*sheni le-tumah*) will not render food unclean, it will not only make water (and other designated liquids) unclean, but will make them a "first level defilement" (*rishon le-tumah*), which can defile foods (Parah 8:7; Pesachim 14b).

Conversely, however, water can cleanse evil at its root. Therefore, in a mikvah, water is needed to cleanse all things.

Water thus involves a joining of good and evil, through which evil can be rectified. Such a joining is referred to as "Knowledge" (Daath), as in the verse, "Adam knew Eve his wife" (Genesis 4:1). The final rectification will take place through the cleansing power of water-knowledge, as it is written, "The world will then be filled with knowledge, as water fills the seas" (Isaiah 11:9).

Since the main rectification of evil is divine reward and punishment, this also comes about through water. It is thus written, "God spreads His light on it, and He covers the depths of the seas; since by these He judges peoples..." (Job 36:30,31; cf. Rashi ad loc.).

When one immerses in a mikvah, one brings oneself back into the hidden saying. In doing so, one totally annuls oneself for God.

As we have seen, a person goes through the ten walls of water through charity. The hidden saying, *Bereshith*, is said to refer to various priestly portions, such as challah, *bikurim*, and *terumah*, all of which are called *reshith* (beginning). This is the concept of

This was a castle made of water.* It had ten walls* one inside the

charity, which is the first money a person must spend. Through charity, one can enter the hidden saying, and thus enter the ten walls of water (*Likutey Halakhoth, Rosh HaShanah* 6:14).

Since water represents knowledge, which is the joining of good and evil, it was the root of the Tree of Knowledge. There are four elements, fire, air, water, and dust, and also four levels of life, humans, animals, plants, and inert objects. The third level is water and plants; therefore, the two are parallel. For this reason, Knowledge was embodied in a tree, which is a member of the plant family. This is also associated with the expansion MaH.

Since water is the joining of good and evil, it is the source of free will. It is also the source of all cleansing.

The fourth level is dust, which corresponds to the expansion BaN. Water is MaH. Indeed, some say that the Hebrew word for water, *mayim,* is the plural of the word *mah,* meaning "what."

It is taught that, at first, God wanted to create the world with the Attribute of Justice. This was BaN, which corresponds to dust, the source of the King's arrows. But God then added the Attribute of Mercy, which is the expansion MaH, and created the world from both. Therefore, the world is created from MaH and BaN, that is, from dust and water. Man was also created from dust and water, and this is why man has free will.

It is written, "the spirit of God hovered over the face of the water" (Genesis 1:2). The Midrash states that this is the "spirit of the Messiah." The Messiah works through the primeval water that came from the hidden saying, and thus will rectify and cleanse the world. But tzaddikim in all generations also participate in this process.

This is why Pharaoh's daughter, when she wanted to escape from the defilement of the palace, went to wash. She wanted to cleanse herself in the concept of water (*Likutey Halakhoth*, Pesach, *Roshay Perakim* 9:3).

The Torah itself is also likened to water, since the Torah is also the means through which evil is elevated and transformed. It is therefore said regarding the Torah, "Let all who thirst come to water" (Isaiah 55:1) (*Likutey Halakhoth, Tolaim* 4:2).

made of water. When the Princess fled, she ran to water. This was the world as it was first created, as the Midrash says, "When the world was first created, it was water in water" (*Yerushalmi, Chagigah* 2:1). Water was the first thing created, and the rest of creation was based on it, as it is written, "God spread the earth on the water" (Psalms 136:6). This indicates that the earth and everything on it originated in water (*Likutey Halakhoth*, Pesach, *Roshay Perakim* 9:2).

The Water Castle is alluded to in the verse, "God will open His good treasury to give you rain in due time" (Deuteronomy 28:12). This good treasury is the Water Castle, which is the source of rain and bounty.

This is why Moses rested by a well after fleeing to Midian (Exodus 2:15). The Midrash states that he was emulating Jacob, who found his wife by a well. All wells pertain to the Water Castle, where the Princess fled. Therefore, Moses and Jacob knew that they would find their aspect of the Princess, that is, a wife, at a well. The Princess includes all virtuous wives.

This is also why Moses was cast into the water as an infant, and then drawn from the water (Exodus 2:3–5). He had to enter through all ten walls of water. This is something that only Moses and the Messiah, the first and last redeemers of Israel, would be able to do. Moses was thus cast into the water to show that he had the ability to pass through the ten walls of water in safety. He could then bring about the redemption, which was the healing of the Princess.

For this reason, the Patriarchs dug wells (Genesis 26:18). Wells are derived from the ten walls of water, where the Malkhuth of holiness is found. This is personified by the Princess, who is faith. Since the Patriarchs saw their task to be revealing faith in God to the world, they dug wells (*Likutey Halakhoth, Rosh HaShanah, Roshay Perakim* 6:3).

As mentioned earlier, the Breaking of the Vessels was through the expansion of BaN, while the rectification is through MaH. Since the four expansions are AB, SaG, MaH, and Ban, and the four elements are fire, air, water, and dust, MaH parallels water, and BaN parallels dust. Therefore, the Breaking of Vessels is associated with dust, while their rectification is through water.

Dust is therefore the place where all the forces of evil have a grasp. It is thus written, "The serpent's bread is dust" (Isaiah 65:25).

Water, on the other hand, cleanses all impurities. It is for this reason that, before entering the Temple or any other holy place, one must immerse in water. Similarly, before a woman can be with her husband, she must immerse. All Israel, similarly, entered the covenant of the Torah through immersion, and a proselyte relives this by immersing in a mikvah (Kerithuth 9a; *Likutey Halakhoth, Tolaim* 4:3).

ten walls. The ten walls of water parallel the ten measures of wisdom given to the world (*Zimrath HaAretz*).

As we have seen, water denotes knowledge and wisdom. Through the ten types of knowledge embodied in the ten walls of water, this beggar could know the ten pulses (*Likutey Halakhoth, Rosh HaShanah, Roshay Perakim* 6:2).

Actually, the ten walls may be alluded to by the fact that the word *water* (*mayim*) occurs eleven times in the account of creation (Genesis 1:2, 1:6 3, 1:7 2, 1:9, 1:10, 1:20, 1:21, l:22). Ten of these parallel the ten sayings with which the world was created, and the eleventh parallels the eleventh saying, "It is not good for man to be alone" (Genesis 2:18), which is the root of evil. These eleven times thus parallel the eleven ingredients in the incense.

Thus, the ten walls parallel the ten sayings of creation (*Avoth* 5:1). The constriction (*tzimtzum*) of God's power that was necessary for creation is represented by the ten walls. The forces of creation involved God's wisdom (Chokhmah), as it is written, "They were all made with wisdom" (Psalms 104:24). Wisdom is represented by water.

Furthermore, the world cannot endure God's wisdom (Chokhmah) unless it is constricted. This constriction is represented by the ten walls of water (*Likutey Halakhoth, Rosh HaShanah, Roshay Perakim* 6:4).

The Ten Walls and Ten Sayings also represent the Ten Sefiroth. These Ten Sefiroth can only be revealed because God constricted His light to the sides, creating a Vacated Space (see *Likutey Moharan* 64). One cannot enter the castle without drowning, since no one can enter the Vacated Space.

All creation was thus constricted from God's wisdom, which is likened to water. Thus, all physical creation also came into being through water. It is thus taught, "at first the universe was water in water" (*Yerushalmi, Chagigah* 2:1). God then created all things from water, as He said, "Let the water be gathered, and let dry land appear" (Genesis 1:9). Therefore, the element of dust also originates from water (see *Sefer Yetzirah*, Long Version 1:12). After that, everything came from dust.

The original light was God's wisdom, which is alluded to by water. The constriction, however, also took place through God's wisdom, and is also water. Therefore, the castle is water, and the walls are also water. This is a paradoxical situation that cannot be understood.

The main creation, however, was the earth, which would be an environment for man. Man was created from "the dust of the earth" (Genesis 2:7). Therefore, the water must be constricted into dust so that we can survive.

We cannot survive on water; similarly, we cannot understand the wisdom (water) and logic of the *tzimtzum* (constriction). But in the Ultimate Future, "The earth will be covered with knowledge of God, just as the water covers the sea" (Isaiah 11:9). We will then understand the wisdom and the logic of the *tzimtzum* (*Likutey Halakhoth, Tolaim* 4:5).

Since the entire *tzimtzum* is alluded to in the word *Bereshith*, this word contains all ten walls of water (*Likutey Halakhoth, Rosh HaShanah* 6:14).

The generation of the flood blemished these ten walls, and, since there was nothing to hold back the water, the flood occurred. Still, the world was not destroyed completely; the walls of the ark remained so that Noah and those with him were able to survive. The Hebrew word for Noah's ark is teyvah, which also has the connotation of a word. This was like the walls of water, which were the ten words or sayings of creation.

When God then swore that He would not send another flood, He showed the rainbow as the sign of His covenant (Genesis 9:13). This bow pertains to the arrows of holiness, which are the antithesis of the arrows of the Evil King. It was seen in the clouds, which are the source of water and rectification. It was also for this reason that the Torah was given in a cloud.

Therefore, in the beginning of the *zikhronoth* (remembrances) on Rosh HaShanah, we recall Noah's ark (*Likutey Halakhoth, Rosh HaShanah, Roshay Perakim* 6:4).

As we have seen, the ten walls of water represent the Vacated Space. Rabbi Nachman teaches that the only way to enter the Vacated Space is through the power of song (*Likutey Moharan* 64). Therefore, the way to enter through these ten walls of water was through the ten types of song (*Chokhmah U'Tevunah* 21:2).

The Torah is likened to water, and the ten walls of water parallel the Ten Commandments, which include the entire Torah. The entire Torah contains 613 commandments, but if one adds up the digits of 613, one obtains 10. This also parallels the ten degrees of prophecy (see *Likutey Moharan Tinyana* 8).

It is impossible to enter the waters of knowledge except through the Torah. The walls are the barriers in the waters of knowledge, which are like the sea; whoever enters them without proper preparation is drowned. This is because there is too much water; there is so much knowledge that one cannot accept it. It is therefore impossible to enter this knowledge to know God. "Too much oil extinguishes the lamp."

The only way one can enter is through faith. This is the power of the Torah, as it is written, "All Your commandments are faith" (Psalms 119:86). Faith is called a wall, as it is written, "I am a wall" (Song of Songs 8:10), and Rashi comments, "My faith is as strong as a wall" (*Likutey Halakhoth, Tolaim* 4:2).

Since the Ten Walls parallel the Ten Sayings of creation, it is fitting that they be mentioned on Rosh HaShanah, which is the time the creation of the world was completed. For this reason, on Rosh HaShanah we recite the psalm, "The earth and everything in it belongs to God, for He founded it on seas ..." (Psalms 24:1-2). This alludes to the Ten Walls upon which the world was founded. These Ten Walls are the constriction of wisdom through which God's essence and kingdom could be revealed (*Likutey Halakhoth, Rosh HaShanah, Roshay Perakim* 6:6).

From Rosh HaShanah until Shemini Atzereth we are engaged in rectifying Malkhuth and faith. As mentioned earlier, during the ten days of repentance, we remove the ten arrows from the Princess (Malkhuth).

Then comes Sukkoth, which alludes to the Clouds of Glory that accompanied the Israelites in the desert. The first mention of cloud came when a "mist arose from the earth and watered the garden" (Genesis 2:6). This was the first "awakening from below." This parallels charity, which causes the clouds to produce rain and water from the ten walls.

All revelation is from cloud. When God gave the Torah, "He spoke to them from a pillar of cloud" (Psalms 99:7). These were clouds of water, which denote knowledge (*Likutey Halakhoth, Rosh HaShanah, Roshay Perakim* 6:4).

The rectification of water was also accomplished on Sukkoth through the water libation (*nisukh ha-mayim*) that was done on this festival. The water went down to the depths, through a channel in the altar known as the *shith*. The Talmud states (*Sukkah* 49a) that this *shith* is alluded to in the word *Bereshith*, which can be broken up into *bara shith*, "He created a *shith*." Thus, the water libations can affect the hidden saying of *Bereshith*. These libations pass through the ten walls of water, to bring up the souls that have fallen through the ten levels of defilement.

While a sacrifice is to refine fallen souls in general, the water libation is meant to raise up the sparks of souls that have fallen into the depths of the realm of evil. They therefore go down to the depths through the *shith,* which is alluded to in the word *Bereshith*, the hidden saying (*Likutey Halakhoth, Rosh HaShanah* 6:14).

The rectification culminates on Shemini Atzereth when we bring the prayers for rain. We want the clouds to bring the right amount of water, and this is regulated by the ten walls. These ten walls stand up through wind, which, as we see, is the song of joy. Since the walls stand up through wind, we first say, "who makes the wind blow," and only then, "who makes the rain fall."

Since the walls are rectified through joy, we pray for rain on Shemini Atzereth, which is a particular time of joy, as it is written, "You shall be only happy" (Deuteronomy 16:15). The second day of Shemini Atzereth is Simchath Torah, when we celebrate the joy of completing the Torah (which is also water on a higher plane) and beginning it again.

other, all made of water. The floors inside this castle were also made of water. This castle also had trees and fruit, all made of water.*

It goes without saying how beautiful this castle was, and how unusual. A castle of water is certainly something wonderful and unusual.

It is impossible for anyone to enter the Water Castle. It is made entirely of water, and anyone entering it would drown.*

Meanwhile, the Queen's Daughter, who had fled to the castle, was going around the Water Castle. The king was informed that she was circling the castle.

The king took his army* and set out to capture her. When the

This joy is the ten types of song. Through these songs, one can hold and balance the ten types of wind, and thus support the ten walls of water, which regulate all rain (*Likutey Halakhoth, Rosh HaShanah, Roshay Perakim* 6:3).

The King's Daughter who fled to the sea represents the entire nation of Israel. The walls of water were therefore like the walls that existed at the splitting of the Red Sea, regarding which it is said, "The water was to them as a wall, to their right and their left" (Exodus 14:22) (*Likutey Halakhoth, Tolaim* 4:4; cf. *Sichoth HaRan* 151).

all made of water. The Water Castle alludes to the Vacated Space that God created in the midst of His Light and Wisdom. As Rabbi Nachman points out, we cannot say that God's wisdom exists in this space, since God vacated it of His wisdom. Yet, we must also say that His wisdom does exist in the space, since the Vacated Space only came into being through God's wisdom. This is a paradox that will not be resolved until the Ultimate Future.

This is like the Water Castle, whose ground, trees, and fruit were all made of water. We cannot find God's wisdom (water) in the Vacated Space, but the space itself is also an aspect of God's wisdom (*Likutey Halakhoth, Tolaim* 4:8).

would drown. The water alludes to wisdom. If one goes into it and does not know one's way one will drown. This is what happened to many philosophers and scientists, who entered the realm of wisdom, but drowned in atheism. This is especially true because, when one is approaching the Water Castle, one is entering the Vacated Space, which contains wisdom that appears to demonstrate the absence of God. But through the power of Torah, one can enter and not be harmed (*Likutey Halakhoth, Tolaim* 4:2).

took his army. When a person flees from the Evil Urge, the Evil Urge gathers all his host and pursues that person. The more a person flees, the more the Evil Urge pursues. That is why, "Whoever is greater has a greater Evil Urge" (*Sukkah* 52a) (*Likutey Halakhoth, Tolaim* 4:2).

On a physical plane this was reenacted by Pharaoh, who pursued the Israelites, taking all his armies (Exodus 14:9; *Likutey Halakhoth, Tolaim* 4:4).

Queen's Daughter saw them coming, she decided that she would flee
into the castle.* She would rather drown than be captured by the king
and have to remain with him. There was also the possibility that she
would survive and be able actually to get into the Water Castle.

When the king saw her fleeing into the water, he said, "If this is
how it is..." and he gave orders to shoot her, saying, "If she dies, she
dies."

The soldiers shot her and hit her with all ten types of arrows,*

flee into the castle. She ran into the Torah, which is likened to water. This is the teaching,
"If you meet the Evil Urge, drag him to the house of Torah study" (*Sukkah* 52b) (*Likutey
Halakhoth, Tolaim* 4:2).

The Torah is life and healing, as it is written, "God's Torah is complete, it restores the
soul" (Psalms 19:8). It can bring a person from the ways of death to the ways of life
(*Likutey Halakhoth, Tolaim* 4:4).

On the physical level, this was represented by Nachshon ben Aminadav, who jumped
into the Red Sea and led the Israelites into the sea to escape Pharaoh.

ten types of arrows. (See *Sichoth HaRan* 273.) These arrows are the Forces of Evil, the
Husks (*klipoth*) and dregs of creation (*Likutey Halakhoth*, Pesach, *Roshay
Perakim* 9:2).

These ten arrows come from the Ten Crowns of Defilement (see *Tikkuney Zohar* 69,
108b; *Likutey Halakhoth, Rosh HaShanah* 6:14).

The King was strong enough that, even though the Princess had run into the water, he
was able to hit her with his arrows. He was able to do so because the rectification
(*tikkun*) is not complete, and there are still 288 sparks of holiness captured among the
forces of evil, giving them strength. It is because of these sparks, that evil can have
power even over the cleansing power of water and Torah. This is also the reason that
water can become defiled very easily, as mentioned earlier. As long as the rectification
(*tikkun*) is not complete, evil has power even there (*Likutey Halakhoth, Tolaim* 4:3).

The fact that the King shoots at her after she has fled into the water, indicates that the
Evil Urge attacks most strongly when people try to immerse themselves in Torah. It is
thus taught that the Evil Urge strikes out against Torah scholars more than anyone else
(*Sukkah* 52a). Although Torah is a protection against the Evil Urge, as soon as the Torah
scholar puts aside his studies, he is particularly vulnerable (*Likutey Halakhoth, Tolaim*
4:2).

These arrows, in particular, represent sexual misdeeds, which are a blemish of the Holy
Covenant of Abraham (*pegam ha-b'rith*). This particularly involves emitting semen in
vain, which injures the Divine Presence like an arrow (*Likutey Moharan* 29). This is
alluded to in the verse "Your arrows have gone deep into me, and Your hand has come
down upon me" (Psalms 38:3) (*Likutey Halakhoth, P'ru U'R'vu* 3:10).

The arrows shot into the Princess are reflected in the sadness and depression that affects
a person. Rabbi Nachman (*Likutey Moharan Tinyana* 24) taught that the main exile of

the Divine Presence comes about primarily through sadness (*Likutey Halakhoth, Rosh HaShanah* 6:8).

This sadness comes from the element of dust (see *Likutey Moharan* 189). This is the advice of the serpent, since "The serpent's bread is dust" (Isaiah 65:25). Moreover, the main power of evil over man is through his illicit sexual urges. The *Zohar* teaches, "The main Evil Urge is illicit sex" (*Zohar* 3:156). This, however, is usually brought about through sadness and depression (*Likutey Halakhoth, Tolaim* 4:2).

As mentioned earlier, the ten arrows come from the Breaking of the Vessels. This comes from the expansion BaN, the lowest of the expansions, paralleling the element of dust. This is also the absence of God from the Vacated Space. But water is the logic of the Vacated Space, which is God's wisdom inside it. This is the beginning of the rectification. The reason the vessels were broken was because the logic and wisdom in the Vacated Space was hidden after the *tzimtzum*. There was some rectification after creation, but it was not complete.

The arrows struck the concept of Malkhuth, which is the Messiah. It is thus written, "He was wounded for our sins" (Isaiah 53:5), which speaks of these arrows. This occurred after the Princess ran into the water, as it is written, "Your breach is like the sea, who will heal you?" (Lamentations 2:13) (*Likutey Halakhoth, Tolaim* 4:8).

These arrows are alluded to at the very beginning of creation, where the Torah says, "The earth was desolute and void, and with darkness on the face of the deep" (Genesis 1:2) (*Likutey Halakhoth*, Pesach, *Roshay Perakim* 9:2).

These arrows of sin are rectified by the arrows of holiness, which denote proper sexuality in a holy context. Regarding this it is written, "Like arrows in the hand of a mighty man, are the children of one's youth" (Psalms 127:4).

Arrows also denote prayer (*Likutey Moharan Tinyana* 83; see *Tikkuney Zohar* 13, 29b). In order to rectify the ten arrows, prayer must be said with a minyan of ten men (*Likutey Halakhoth, Rosh HaShanah, Roshay Perakim* 6:4).

The Princess absorbing the arrows was also paralleled by the angel absorbing the arrows that the Egyptians shot at the time of the Exodus. Regarding this it is written, "The angel of God which went before the camp of Israel, moved and went behind them, and the pillar of cloud moved from behind them, and stood between them, coming between the camp of Egypt and the camp of Israel" (Exodus 14:19, 20). Rashi notes that it came between the two camps to absorb the arrows that the Egyptians were shooting at the Israelites. This "cloud" represented the Shekhinah, which absorbed the ten arrows of the Evil King.

The battle down below was a counterpart of the war on high. Just as the Egyptians were firing arrows down below, the Evil One was firing his arrows on high. These arrows were arrows of doubt and disbelief, causing the Israelites to rebel against God. It is thus written, "They rebelled at the Red Sea, they crossed a sea of woes" (Psalms 106:7; Zechariah 10:11).

As a result of these ten arrows, the Israelites were injured spiritually, so that they rebelled against God ten times in the desert (*Avoth* 5:4). We are still not healed from the effects of these arrows. From them, all heresy and doubt come. It is thus written, "The wicked bent the bow, they made their arrow ready on the string, that they may shoot the

rubbed with the ten types of poison. She ran into the castle,* and entered into it. She went through the gates in the walls of water. The walls of water have such gates. She passed through all ten walls of the Water Castle, until she came to its interior. When she got there, she fell unconscious.*

I heal her.* Someone who does not possess* all ten types of char-

upright in the heart with darkness" (Psalms 11:2).

It would have been utterly impossible for the Princess to tolerate the poison arrows so long if God had not made the remedy before the sickness, helping her to flee into the ten walls of water. These represent the Torah, which is life and healing (*Likutey Halakhoth, Tolaim* 4:4).

The arrows are therefore shot only after the Princess runs into the sea. This was alluded to when, in the first plague, the water turned into blood. God then took the Israelites through the sea to escape the Egyptians. The King attacked the Israelites in the sea at the very beginning, too, by having all their sons cast into the Nile. Moses had to be cast into the Nile as well, since he would have to enter the ten walls of water to heal the Princess (*Likutey Halakhoth, Pesach, Roshay Perakim* 9:3).

ran into the castle. Her running into the Water Castle represents the Israelites fleeing evil by immersing themselves in the Torah. Torah is life and healing, as it is written, "God's Torah is complete, it restores the soul" (Psalms 19:8). When the Israelites run to the Torah, they have the power to tolerate the exile, which is a result of the ten arrows. It is thus written, "The Torah is your life and the length of your days" (Deuteronomy 30:20) (*Likutey Halakhoth, Tolaim* 4:4).

However, even though she ran into the water, the arrows hit her. Even though water is purification, it was not entirely rectified. Therefore, it did not offer complete protection against the arrows (*Likutey Halakhoth, Tolaim* 4:8).

unconscious. The Israelites are weary and faint because of their sins (*Sichoth HaRan* 273).

The fainting of the Princess is alluded to by "the darkness on the face of the deep" (Genesis 1:2). She almost died, but was sustained by the spirit of the Messiah. The verse thus continues, "The spirit of God hovered on the face of the waters" (ibid.) and the Midrash states that this is the spirit of the Messiah. Kabbalistically, this also represents the sparks of holiness that give life force to everything that has fallen into the *klipoth*. In a sense, it is the Messianic hope that gives hope even to those who have fallen into the lowest realms of evil (*Likutey Halakhoth, Tolaim* 4:3; cf. *Likutey Halakhoth, Pesach, Roshay Perakim* 9:2).

The Princess would remain unconscious in the Water Castle for hundreds of years (*Likutey Halakhoth, P'ru U'R'vu* 3:10).

Some say that the reason she fainted was because the walls of water were not completely rectified; therefore, there was too much light (*Chokhmah U'Tevunah* 21:2).

I heal her. Only a great tzaddik, who has the power to enter every place where the soul has fallen, and remove all ten arrows, can heal the Princess (*Sichoth HaRan* 273). Of

ity cannot enter all ten walls; he will drown* in the water there. The king and his army tried to pursue her, but they all drowned* in the water. I, on the other hand, was able* to go through all ten walls of water.

These walls of water are like the waves of the sea which stand like a wall.* The winds support the waves* and lift them up. These waves constitute the ten walls which stand there permanently,* but they are lifted up and supported by the winds. I, however, was able to enter through all ten walls.

I was also able to draw all ten types of arrows* out of the Queen's Daughter. I also knew all ten types of pulses,* and could detect them

course, the final healing will be accomplished by the Messiah (*Likutey Halakhoth, Tolaim* 4:4).

possess. Literally, "have in his hands," alluding to the power of the hands.

he will drown. If a person has a tradition from his master, he can enter all ten walls without being harmed. But if he does not, he can drown. This refers to the walls of water of wisdom, which can drown a person in atheism and heresy. This is what happened to many philosophers and scientists (*Likutey Halakhoth, Tolaim* 4:2).

they all drowned. Just as Pharaoh and his army drowned when they pursued the Israelites into the Red Sea (Exodus 14:28; *Likutey Halakhoth, Tolaim* 4:4).

was able. This is alluded to in the verse, "The spirit of God hovered on the face of the waters" (Genesis 1:2). This is the spirit of the Messiah, which entered into the water where the Princess had fled (*Likutey Halakhoth*, Pesach, *Roshay Perakim* 9:2; *Likutey Halakhoth, Tolaim* 4:3).

stand like a wall. They stand up through the wind, which denotes joy (*Likutey Halakhoth*, Rosh HaShanah, *Roshay Perakim* 6:3).

winds support the waves. Alluded to in the verse, "Your charity is like the waves of the sea" (Isaiah 48:18) (end of story).

stand there permanently. The walls stand up through the same spirit-wind that produces the pulse beat. The wind of song also gives strength to the wind of the pulse. Hence, everything depends on song. This is the level of cantillations (*taamim*), which is the highest of the four levels (*Likutey Halakhoth, Tolaim* 4:11).

all ten types of arrows. Taking out the arrows is the process of purification, transforming uncleanness into purity. It is the task of all the Israelites, and especially the tzaddikim, to remove these arrows (*Likutey Halakhoth*, Pesach, *Roshay Perakim* 9:2).

all ten types of pulses. So that he can recognize the spiritual sickness of each and every person (*Likutey Halakhoth, Tolaim* 4:2).

with my ten fingers. Each one of the ten fingers has the power to detect one of the ten types of pulse. I could then heal her through the ten types of melody.*

I thus heal her.* Therefore, I have this great power in my hands.* I am now giving you this as a gift.

through the ten types of melody. This healing is primarily through joy. It is thus written regarding the Messianic age, "It is good to give thanks to God ... with a ten stringed instrument (denoting the ten songs), with a lute, with meditation on the harp. For You, God, have made me happy through Your works" (Psalms 92:1–5).

The joy of these ten types of songs comes through the Ten Psalms of the Tikkun HaKelali. Defilement of Abraham's covenant (sexual misdeeds) comes as a result of sadness. Therefore, when "all flesh had corrupted their way" (Genesis 6:12) through sexual immorality, God "was saddened through His heart" (Genesis 6:6). The covenant is therefore rectified through joy (*Likutey Halakhoth, Tolaim* 4:2).

The ten types of songs are included in the Song of the Red Sea, which, according to the Talmud (*Sanhedrin* 91b), Moses will sing in the Messianic age. Therefore, the song literally begins, "Then Moses will sing" (Exodus 15:1). The Messiah is an aspect of Moses, and when he comes, he will sing this song which includes all ten songs, and the Shekhinah will be healed. Regarding this it is written, "Sing to God a new song, for He has done wonders" (Psalms 98:1).

The song of the Red Sea ends, "God will reign forever and ever" (Exodus 15:18). This is speaking of God's kingdom in the Messianic age, when the attribute of Malkhuth (royalty, the Princess) will be rectified. Regarding this it is written, "Let the heavens rejoice and earth be glad, and let nations say,"God is King" (Psalms 96:11). Then we will, "Sing to God, sing to our King, for God is King of all the earth" (Psalms 47:7).

The Princess is thus healed primarily through song. It is thus written, "Praise God with the harp, with a lyre of ten (songs); sing to Him, sing to Him a new song" (Psalms 33:2) (*Likutey Halakhoth, Tolaim* 4:4).

I thus heal her. It is thus written, "Is there no balm in Gilead? Is there no physician there? Why then is the daughter of my people not healed?" (Jeremiah 8:22). God likewise says, "I have stricken down and I will heal" (Deuteronomy 32:39) in the Ultimate Future. The commentaries note that God heals with the same thing with which He strikes, this being the concept of shooting the arrow and then retrieving it. This is the concept of rectifying evil at its very root (*Likutey Halakhoth, Tolaim* 4:8).

The Princess can thus be healed only through a very great tzaddik (*Likutey Etzoth* B, *Tzaddik* 96). However, the final healing of the Princess is the final redemption, regarding which it is said, "On that day, God will heal His people's wound, and heal them of their bruise" (Isaiah 30:26) (*Kedushath Shabbath*).

power in my hands. Like the story of the fourth day, the story of the sixth day is not completed. This is a process that is still ongoing. However, when other people realize how far they are from the handless beggar, the rectification can be complete (*Rimzey Maasioth*).

When he finished his speech, there was great joy and tremendous rejoicing.

Rabbi Nachman concluded:
It is very difficult for me to tell this story. However, since I have begun it, I am forced to end it. There is not a single redundant word in this story. One who is versed in the sacred literature will be able to understand some of the allusions.

The story speaks of arrows, and a certain power in the hands to turn back arrows. This is related to God's statement, "My hand will grasp judgment" (Deuteronomy 32:41). Rashi explains this verse saying, "When a human being shoots an arrow, he cannot turn it back, but when God shoots an arrow, He can."

The concept of charity is seen as being related to the walls of water, which are the waves of the sea. This is alluded to in the verse, "Your charity is like the waves of the sea" (Isaiah 48:18).

The story speaks of the power of grasping the winds in one's hand. This is alluded to in the verse, "Who gathers up the wind in His palm" (Proverbs 30:4). This is related to the concept of melody as mentioned elsewhere (*Likutey Moharan* I 54).

The ten types of melody and ten types of pulses have been discussed earlier.*

Rabbi Nathan adds:
All this I heard explicitly. However, regarding the meaning of who, what and when, the story is very deep. This involves the primary concept of the story itself. Who were the beggars? What were they? When were they? All this is too deep to be understood.

---

discussed earlier. The source cites *Likutey Moharan Tinyana* p. 32a. This reference denotes the first edition of the second part of *Likutey Moharan* (Mohalov, 1811). The reference is to *Likutey Moharan Tinyana* 92.

Rabbi Nathan continues:
The end of the story would involve the Seventh Day* and the beggar without feet.* However, we were not worthy of hearing it. The same is true of the end of the first part of the story, regarding the king who gave over his kingdom to his son during his lifetime. Rabbi Nachman said that he would not tell any more. This is a great loss. We will not be worthy of hearing it until the Messiah comes.* May this happen quickly in our days, Amen.

Rabbi Nachman also said, "If I knew nothing else other than this story, it would still be very extraordinary."*

the Seventh Day. A group was standing around Rabbi Nachman after he finished the story of the sixth day, and someone told him an anecdote. He said, "This is the story of the seventh day. It seems that people are already telling my story. I would very much like to finish it." However, the story was never finished (*Sichoth HaRan* 149; cf. ibid. 151; *Yemey Moharnat*, p. 32b).

This story would involve the beggar without feet. From the lessons of Rabbi Nachman, it seems that his power would be through dancing. Rabbi Nachman thus taught that by dancing with one's feet, one can restore lost faith (*Likutey Moharan Tinyana* 81). However, in the beginning of the story, Rabbi Nachman told how the King's Son had lost his faith. Thus, the story of the seventh day, might involve the restoration of this faith (*Chokhmah U'Tevunah* 15:1).

beggar without feet. The time before the Messiah is known as *Ikvatha deMeshicha*, which literally means "the heels of the Messiah." Therefore, the power of rectification of the Messiah comes from his feet.

This is related to the story of the Prince at the beginning of this story. The king tells him that the main thing is joy, which is expressed by the feet in dancing. In the World to Come, it is taught that God will make a dance for all the righteous. All of them will then point to God and say, "This is God, I have hoped for Him" (Isaiah 25:9; *Taanith* 31a). This is the concept of the complete restoration of faith (*Chokhmah U'Tevunah*).

The beggar with no feet is the one who will effect the ultimate rectification of the Princess, who is the Shekhinah. Regarding the Shekhinah it is written, "Her feet go down to death" (Proverbs 5:5). This is because the feet of Malkhuth go down to the realm of evil, giving it existence until the Messiah comes and rectifies all things. Thus, the ultimate rectification is through the feet.

until the Messiah comes. When Rabbi Nachman left Breslov for good and was traveling to Uman, he said that we would not be worthy of hearing the end of the story until the Messiah came (*Yemey Moharnat*, p. 32b).

very extraordinary. Elsewhere, this is presented as, "If I only told the world this one story, I would still be very great" (*Likutey Halakhoth, Tefillin* 5:1). He indicated that this story

He said explicitly that this story is wonderful and unusual. It contains many moral lessons and Torah lessons, and has in it many Torah concepts and many teachings.

It also speaks of many ancient saints. Thus, King David stood at one end of the earth, and screamed out to the spring which issues forth

contains many lessons regarding many ancient tzaddikim (*Likutey Halakhoth, Evven HaEzer, P'ru U'R'vu* 3:10).

The following appears after the story in Hebrew:

The concept of King David and the above mentioned verse "From the ends of the earth" which alludes to the story. This pertains to the third day, for there they spoke about the Heart and the Spring. See there. And you will see wonders, how in each concept wondrous things are alluded to. Of the great awesome things of this story it is impossible to speak at all, for this is above all. Happy, happy is he who is worthy, even in the World to Come, of understanding a little of it. If a person has any brain, his hair will stand on end when he looks well at this awesome story; and he will understand a little of the greatness of the Creator and the greatness of the true tzaddikim, for nothing like it has ever been heard.

I heard the concept of the verse "From the ends of the earth..." mentioned above, which pertains to the story of the third day, explicitly from the Rebbe's holy, awesome lips (may he rest in peace). I also found that most of the words of this Psalm 61 in which this verse is written, allude to lofty mysteries of the story of the third day. "Days on the days of the king shall be increased..." because he constantly needs that days should be added on his days ... as mentioned above.

"Kindness and truth will preserve him" (Psalms 61:8). This is the true man of kindness ... *der groiser man der emeser ish chesed*. For all time and days are made through the great man, who is a true man of kindness, as noted in the story. He continues and increases the "days of the king." This is the Heart mentioned above, which is the concept of King David, and this is the meaning of "he will preserve him." He watches and preserves it so that as soon as it comes very close to the end of the day when the Heart of all the world would die, then this true man of kindness protects and watches it, when he comes and gives a day to the Heart...

And this is the meaning of "Thus I will sing to Your name forever to pay my vows of each day" (Psalms 61:9). For every day that he gives comes from the hymns and songs. "I will take refuge in the cover of Your wings selah" (Psalms 61:5). When the Heart needs to rest, the Great Bird comes and spreads its wings over it... This is "I will take refuge in the cover of Your wings..."

This pertains to the first day, the concept of the old men. Each one boasted about what he remembered. One remembered even when they cut his navel ... and he was the least of them...

The Rebbe, of blessed memory, said that in the Talmud there is a similar concept where Shmuel boasted that he remembered the pain of circumcision... (*Yerushalmi Kethuboth* 5).

from the stone on the mountain. It is thus written, "From the ends of the earth, I call to You. When my heart is faint, lead me to a rock that is too high for me" (Psalms 61:3).

All this, I heard from Rabbi Nachman's own mouth explicitly. From his words, it is obvious that King David is the heart mentioned in the story, where the heart of the world stands at one end of the world facing the spring, and screams out in constant desire... Still the ideas are obscure. Happy is he who is worthy of grasping the mystery of these stories.

2   The Chandelier*

Once a son left his father, and remained in a distant land for many years. When he returned home, he boasted about how he had learned the art of making chandeliers.* He told his father to invite all the local masters of this craft, so that he could demonstrate his skill.

His father invited all the masters of the craft to see the skills that his son had learned during the time he was away. However, when the son took out a lamp that he had made, they all realized that it was very ugly. The father later went to them, and asked them to tell him the truth. Since they had no choice but to tell the truth, they told him that the lamp was very ugly.

Later the son boasted to his father, "Didn't you see the wisdom of my craft?"

The father replied that the other craftsmen considered it to be very inferior work.

The son replied, "They have it backwards. Through this lamp, I have demonstrated my skill. I have shown each one of them his shortcomings. In this lamp, I included the shortcomings of all the local masters of this art. You did not realize that one considered one part ugly, but another part very well made. The next one, however, considered the first part beautiful and wonderful, while for him, the second part was poorly made.

"This is true of all of them. What one considers bad, is good to another, and vice versa.

"I made this lamp out of shortcomings and nothing else, to demonstrate to all of them that they do not have perfection. Each one has a shortcoming, since what is beautiful to one is deficient to the next.

The Chandelier. This and subsequent stories are only in Hebrew.

chandeliers. *Heng leichter* in Yiddish.

But if I want to, I can make a perfect lamp."*

If people knew all the shortcomings and deficiencies in a thing, they would know the essential nature of that thing, even if they had never seen it before.

"Great are God's deeds" (Psalms 111:2). No man resembles another. Adam had every human form in the world. Moreover, the Hebrew word for man, *adam*, includes all these forms. The same is true of all other things. In the Hebrew word for light, *or*, all lights are included.

The same is true of everything else in creation. Even in a forest, no two leaves are alike.

Rabbi Nachman spoke of this at length. He then said, "Types of wisdom exist* that can sustain a person completely. A person could live with such wisdom, without eating or drinking." He then spoke at length of this awesome concept.

I can make a perfect lamp. Thus, the Land of Israel is perfect; it lacks nothing. It is thus described as, "A land in which you will lack nothing" (Deuteronomy 8:9). If one sees any shortcomings in the land, it is merely because of one's own deficiencies, which prevent one from recognizing its good. The *Sifri* thus says that everything that the spies (*meraglim*) saw as shortcomings in the land were actually advantages (*Zimrath HaAretz*).

Types of wisdom exist... Another time, Rabbi Nachman said, "I know wisdom that cannot be revealed. If I were to reveal this wisdom, people would be nourished by the delight of comprehending it, and they would no longer eat or drink. Every soul in the world would long to hear this wisdom, and everything in the world would stop. People would seek the sweet beauty of this wisdom, and would leave this mundane life. But I cannot reveal this wisdom to mankind. As soon as I begin to speak of it, I hear lofty things in the words of the listener. I then stop speaking so that I can listen and receive from him" (*Sichoth HaRan* 181).

He also said, "There are categories of wisdom, even in this physical world, which can sustain a person without any other nourishment. Such awesome, wonderful categories of wisdom exist even in the mundane world. With this wisdom alone, a person could live without eating or drinking" (*Sichoth HaRan* 306).

Rabbi Nachman's follower, Rabbi Naftali, told that once the Rebbe's mother asked him, "Why do you push yourself not to eat? With what will you live?"

Rabbi Nachman replied, "I now live with 'wisdom gives life to its owners'" (Ecclesiastes 7:12).

He also said, "I have men with me who know things with which they can live without eating or drinking" (*Shevachey Moharan* 3b 9).

The *Zohar* thus speaks of "being nourished by the radiance of the Divine."

3   The Horse and the Pump*

Rabbi Nachman's followers spoke of a person who was in a large gentile city, and remained there a long time. He was trying to reach a certain goal there, and each time, it appeared as if he would accomplish it. But in the end he remained there a very long time.

Rabbi Nachman said that this often happens to people. Each time a person thinks that he will accomplish something. He says, "Now I will accomplish it." Then later, "Now I will finally accomplish it." This goes on and on.

Once there was a man who did not believe in *letzim* (jokers).* These are demons from the Other Side, who sometimes come and lead people astray. Although there have been many encounters with such beings, this man did not believe in them.

One night a *letz* (joker) came to him and called him, asking him to come outside. When he went outside, the *letz* showed him a beautiful horse that he had to sell. Examining it, he saw that it was indeed a very beautiful animal. "How much do you want for it?" he asked.

"Four rubles,"* replied the *letz*.

The man realized that the horse was worth at least* eight rubles. It was a prime horse in very good condition. He bought the horse for four rubles, and felt that he had got an excellent bargain.

The Horse and the Pump. Rabbi Nachman told this story on Shavuoth, 5567 (Friday, June 12, 1807) (*Chayay Moharan* 15d, 59). Rabbi Nachman had taken his fateful journey to Navritch, and his wife had died in Zaslev just before Shavuoth. That Friday night, Rabbi Nachman put on his shtreimel for the first time that festival. He then sat until morning with Rabbi Nathan and a few other men. It was then that he told this story (*Yemey Moharnat* 19b, 20a).

letzim. Jokers. Apparently these are a type of poltergeist (see *Kav HaYashar* 69).

rubles. *Adumim* in Hebrew.

at least. Approximately, *be-shufi* in Hebrew.

87

The next day, he took out the horse to sell it. People came, and immediately wanted to give him the asking price. He said to himself, "If they want to give me that much, it is obviously worth twice as much." Therefore, he refused to sell it.

He brought the horse elsewhere, and people were ready to give him twice his original price. He said to himself, "Most probably, it is worth more than twice this amount."

He kept on bringing the horse further and further, until its price was in the thousands. He still would not agree to sell it to anyone, no matter how much he was offered. He always said, "Most probably it's worth twice as much." Finally, he could not find anyone who could afford it other than the king.

When he brought the horse to the king, the king offered him a huge sum of money for it. Everyone agreed that it was a very fine horse. However, he could not come to an agreement with the king, since he said, "Most probably it is worth even more." Thus, even the king could not buy the horse from him.

He left the king, and brought the horse to a pump to give it water. The horse immediately jumped into the pump and vanished. Of course, this was only an illusion made by the *letzim*. The entire horse was such an illusion, and they made the horse appear to jump into the pump.

The man began to scream because of what had happened, and people heard the screams and gathered around him. "Why are you screaming?" they asked.

He replied that his horse had jumped into the pump.

The people hit him and beat him; they thought he was mad. The pump's opening was very small. How could a horse possibly jump into it?

He realized that they were beating him because he appeared to be a madman, and he wanted to leave. Just as he was preparing to leave, however, the horse stuck its head out of the pump. Thinking that he had his horse, he began to scream again.* Again the townspeople gathered around him and beat him as a madman.

---

scream again. "Hah! Hah!" in the source.

Again he wanted to leave, but as soon as he was preparing to leave, the horse stuck its head out of the pump. He began to scream again, and again the people gathered and beat him.

The Other Side constantly fools a person for no reason, with absolute falsehood that does not have any substance. The person is tempted, and goes after it. Each time it appears that he will make more profit, and he desires all the more. He pursues it many times, and suddenly it vanishes. As he runs after it, everything he desires is taken away from him.

Sometimes, the desire goes away a little. But when he wants to separate himself from it completely, the desire sticks out its head again, and once again he pursues it. This keeps on happening. Every time it sticks out its head, he runs after it.

Rabbi Nachman did not explain this concept further. Understand it well.

*

There was once a great saint, who had completely overcome his sexual desires. When he had perfected himself sexually, he ascended to the highest worlds. There he saw a pot full of flesh and bones.

"What is this?" he asked.

He was told, "This was once an extremely beautiful woman. But she would warm up her body to sin. Therefore, she is being 'warmed' here in this pot."

He wanted to see what she looked like. He was given Divine Names, so that he was able to reassemble her as she was during life. He saw that she was a very great beauty.

From this, we can see how improper this type of desire is. If a woman were cut into little pieces, how much desire would be left for her?

4   The Melancholy Saint

Sadness is a very despicable trait. One must keep oneself from it completely. One must encourage and uplift oneself. A person must realize that every time he makes even the slightest motion to serve God, it is very precious in God's eyes. This is true even if that person only moves himself by a single hairsbreadth.

This is because a person exists in a physical body in the lowest of the worlds. Therefore, every movement is extremely difficult for him, and is very precious in God's eyes.

There was once a tzaddik who became very depressed and melancholy.* This depression and melancholy caused the tzaddik great difficulty, and it became worse and worse. He fell into lassitude and heaviness, where it was literally impossible for him to move.

He wanted to make himself happy and uplift himself, but it was impossible for him to do anything. Whenever he found something that would make him happy, the Evil One would find sadness in it. Therefore, it was impossible for him to do anything to make himself happy, since in everything he found sadness.

---

depressed and melancholy. This is the version that Rabbi Nathan heard. Another of Rabbi Nachman's followers heard the following version: There was a tzaddik who felt that he had to serve God perfectly each day. He calculated exactly what he had to do, down to the number of steps he would take each day in his house. When things did not work out as he planned, he became very depressed (*Chayay Moharan*, p. 16b 6).

The main reason a person becomes depressed is because he is proud. He therefore feels that he should be able to accomplish much more than he does. But in the end the tzaddik realizes that the only thing that can make him happy is the fact that God did not create him as a gentile, which was something over which he had no control. He was then humble, and this led to joy, as it is written, "The humble shall have increased joy in God" (Isaiah 29:19). It is also written, "The humble shall listen and rejoice" (Psalms 34:3), and "The humble will see and rejoice" (Psalms 59:33) (*Likutey Halakhoth*, Pesach 9:15).

Finally the tzaddik began to meditate* on the fact that God had not created him* as a heathen. This could certainly be the source of unlimited joy. It is impossible even to imagine the thousands of levels of separation between the lowest possible Israelite and the unclean spiritual level of the idolator.

He pondered God's kindness that "He did not make me a heathen" and realized that this could be a source of great joy, without any sadness.*

When a person tries to find joy in something that he himself did, it is possible to find sadness in every joy. No matter what he does, he can find shortcomings, and he will not be able to uplift himself and be happy. But in the fact that "He did not make me a heathen," there is no sadness. This is from God; God made him the way He did, and had pity on him, not making him a heathen. Since this was God's deed, there are no shortcomings in it, and hence there is no defect in this rejoicing. No matter what, there is an unimaginable difference between him and an idolator.

The tzaddik began to make himself happy with this. He rejoiced and uplifted himself little by little, continuing more and more, until he came to such a level of joy that he was on the same level of joy that Moses experienced when he went on high to receive the Tablets.

Through this uplifting and joy, he was able to fly many miles into the supernal universes. He saw himself, and he was very far from the place where he had been originally. This bothered him very much. He felt that when he descended, he would be very far away from his original place.

---

began to meditate... When a person is on the lowest level, it is easy for him to find something with which to uplift himself (*Likutey Halakhoth, Yoreh Deah, Reshith HaGez* 4:6).

had not created him... *Shelo asani goy* (in the first person). This is the wording of one of the morning blessings.

joy, without any sadness. The main thing, then, is to make a small beginning. God thus said, "Open for Me like the eye of a needle, and I will open for you like the gates of the Temple" (*Shir HaShirim Rabbah* 5:3) (*Oneg Shabbath*, p. 48).

Thus, no matter how low a person is, if he makes even a single motion to serve God, it is something very great on high, and it can bring him back completely (*Likutey Halakhoth, Tefillin* 5:43).

The main thing is to make the first move. If one begins even a little bit, one can go very high (*Parparoth LeChokhmah* 6:8).

When it was discovered that he had disappeared, people would consider it a great wonder. The tzaddik did not want such publicity since he always wanted to "walk modestly with God" (Micah 6:8).

The joy came to an end, since joy has a limit. Therefore, joy begins automatically and ends automatically. When joy begins to end, it ends little by little. The tzaddik therefore descended little by little, coming down from the place to which he had flown during his time of joy. He eventually returned to the place from which he had ascended. He was very surprised, since he was in exactly the same place where he had been at first.

He realized that he had returned to the exact same place where he had been at first. Looking at himself, he realized that the had not moved at all, or if he had moved, it had been at most by a hairsbreadth.* He had moved so little, that no one other than God could measure it. The tzaddik was very surprised at this. Here he had flown so far, through so many universes, and at the same time, he had not moved at all.

This showed him how precious in God's eyes is even the slightest motion. When a person moves himself even a hairsbreadth in this world, it can be considered more than thousands of miles, and even thousands of universes.

This can be understood, when we realize that the physical world is no more than the central point* in the midst of the spheres.* This is

---

hairsbreadth. The hair on the head is the gate to the intellect. In Hebrew, the word *sa'ar* meaning hair, and *sha'ar* meaning gate, are the same. Therefore, if a person improves himself by a hairsbreadth, it can bring him back completely. Similarly, if a person strays from God by a hairsbreadth, it can do much damage (*Likutey Halakhoth, Choshen Mishpat*, Nezikin 4:3).

For this reason, even the smallest amount of leaven (*chametz*) is forbidden on Pesach. *Chametz* represents the side of evil, and even the smallest amount is extremely harmful (*Likutey Halakhoth*, Nezikin 4:4).

central point. Therefore, the physical earth upon which we walk is the ultimate constriction (*tzimtzum*). Wherever a person walks, he comes to other points, where there is a different *tzimtzum*. Therefore, traveling and doing good brings Godliness into new areas of *tzimtzum*. For this reason, the Israelites traveled for forty years in the desert. With every step, they created new faith, thus rectifying Adam's sin (*Likutey Halakhoth, Eruv Tavshilin* 5:20).

spheres. The orbits of the planets around the earth. This takes a relativistic geocentric view of the universe.

known to masters of astronomy. Compared to the supernal universes, the entire physical universe is no more than a dot.

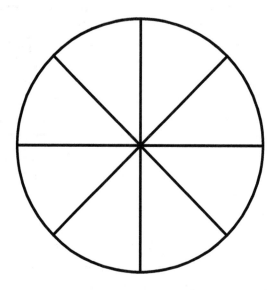

When lines extend from a central point, the closer they are to the point, the closer they are to one another. The further they extend from the point, the further such lines get from each other. Therefore, when the lines are very far from the point, they are also very far from each other. This is true, even though near the central point, they are extremely close to each other.

If one imagined lines drawn from the earth to the upper spheres,* one would see that even if one moved a hairsbreadth, the movement would be reflected as a motion of thousands of miles in the upper spheres. It would be in the same ratio as the spheres are higher than the earth. The spheres must be very huge, since there are stars without number, and each star is at least as large as our planet.

---

to the upper spheres. Therefore, even holiness that is like a hairsbreadth down below is more precious than millions of universes on high (*Likutey Halakhoth, Chol HaMoed* 4:13). Since a person lives in a physical body, and has many obstacles in the physical world, moving away from evil by even a hairsbreadth is something very precious to God (*Likutey Halakhoth, Yoreh Deah, Reshith HaGez* 4:1).

This is all the more certainly true when one considers the supernal universe, compared to which, even the highest astronomical spheres are like nothing. Therefore, the distance between these extending lines in the supernal world is without measure. A movement of less than a hairsbreadth, so small that only God can estimate it, can consist of a passage through thousands of universes and thousands of miles in the supernal worlds.

How much more is this true when one travels a mile or more to serve God. "No eye has seen it..." (Isaiah 64:3).

5   Two Palaces*

There are two types of palaces, and the two are very much the same. However, in one a king lives, and in the other, a slave lives. Obviously, there is a great difference between the palace of the king and the palace of the slave. Nevertheless, it is possible to confuse the two.

This is because there is a knot that binds many souls together, until a house and palace are made from them. One is bound to another, and one to another, until they make a foundation. Then a tent is made, until finally, out of them are built a house and a dwelling place.

This dwelling place is a habitation for truth. When one needs to seek the truth, it can be found in that dwelling place, made of the knots of souls. They make up the dwelling place of truth.

It is for this reason that the Torah commands, "Incline after the majority" (Exodus 23:2). Since many are bound together, it is a place of truth.

This is also the concept of, "All the souls of the house of Jacob" (Genesis 46:27). This teaches that out of the souls, the house of Jacob was made. This is the house and dwelling place of truth, which is Jacob's quality, as it is written, "You will give truth to Jacob" (Micah 7:20).

Opposing this, however, is the knot of the wicked, where the souls of many wicked are bound together to form a house and dwelling place for falsehood. Regarding this, the prophet warned, "Do not say that everything that people call a knot (conspiracy) is a knot" (Isaiah 8:12).

The knot of the wicked does not count. Regarding it, it is written, "Do not follow the multitude to do evil" (Exodus 23:2).

It is possible, however, to confuse the two houses, confusing truth

---

Two Palaces. This is related to the story of "The Exchanged Children" (see The Lost Princess). The king's son can forget his status to such an extent that even he cannot discern between the two palaces (Likutey Halakhoth, Birkath HaShachar 3:11).

and falsehood. Falsehood often disguises itself as truth. In falsehood there is also a knot of many souls. Therefore, it is possible for a person to be mistaken and confused, and not know where the truth is. He then does not know what group to join.

However, through the commandment of redeeming captives* (*pidyon shevuyim*), one is worthy of discerning between the two houses, between truth and falsehood, and between the king and the slave. Falsehood is the concept of the slave and the concept of the accursed.* This is the concept of "Cursed is Canaan, he shall be a slave of slaves" (Genesis 9:25).

There are two types of intelligence. They are an aspect of "before and after" (Psalms 139:5).

There is a type of intelligence that comes to a person in the course of time. The older he becomes, the more he knows. This is the concept of "days speak" (Job 32:7). This type of intelligence is an aspect of "after," since it comes *after* time has elapsed. For such intelligence, time is needed.

But there is a type of intelligence that comes to a person as a sudden influx (*shefa*) in an instant. This type of intelligence is higher than time, and does not need any time to develop. This intelligence is an aspect of "before." In Hebrew, this is *panim*, which also means "face." This is the concept of Jacob, and the concept of the truth, alluded to in the verse, "They seek your face, Jacob, Selah" (Psalms 24:6).

After the Sabbath of the portion of *VaYechi*, Rabbi Nachman said: At the third meal (*Shalosh Seudoth*), there was revealed to me a specific remedy (*segulah*) for the pox.* Take some chalk.* Then take an

---

redeeming captives. Captives are like slaves. Therefore, when they are redeemed, they are brought out of the aspect of being slaves (*Chayay Moharan* 16c 7).

accursed. Even if a man serves God, but he is still a slave, he is accursed. However, there is also a concept of a holy slave, such as that of "Moses, God's slave" (Deuteronomy 34:5; see *Likutey Moharan* 5).

pox. *Pakin* in Yiddish.

chalk. *Kreid* in Yiddish. The word also denotes lime or whiting.

amount of soap weighing three times as much as the chalk. Make a bath from both of them, and bathe the infant. This must be done as soon as the child begins to have a fever. If there is not a powerful decree against the child, it will be successful. However, if it is a powerful decree, heaven forbid, then it will not help.

Pox is a result of the sin of the Golden Calf.

It may be difficult to understand this, since gentiles are also affected by this disease. However, the Midrash teaches that the gentiles really should not be affected by any sickness, since the physical world is their portion. But so that they would not denigrate the Israelites, God gave them all the sicknesses that the Israelites have.

Rashi expresses a similar thought in his commentary on the verse, "Make me not a reproach for the degraded ones" (Psalms 39:9). The prayer was that the degraded ones should also be stricken with disease and pain, so that they would not be able to say, "You are stricken and we are not stricken." This prayer caused pain and sickness to come to the gentiles.

Another difficulty arises because this sickness must have also existed before the sin of the Golden Calf. However, before that time, it was not a serious illness. Pox results from the food that the infant absorbs in its mother's womb, as physicians say. However, it was originally not a fatal illness as it is now. This was caused by the sin.

This is alluded to in some degree in the verse, "You may wash yourselves with *nether*, and use very much *borith*, but your sin is still written before Me" (Jeremiah 2:22). Rashi explains that the sin in this verse is the sin of the Golden Calf.

Nether is chalk. *Borith* is soap.

(Therefore, this verse alludes to a specific remedy for an illness that comes because of the sin of the Golden Calf. It must be washed away with *nether*, which is chalk or lime, along with a greater portion of *borith*, which is soap.) Understand the wonders here.

From the days of Rabbi Nachman's youth:
Once people came to him with a redemption (*pidyon*), asking that he pray for a child by the name of Sarah Esther *bat* Yehudith. He said that she would die, and she did.

He said that he knew this from the Torah itself. It is written, "The fish that were in the Nile died and stank" (Exodus 7:21). The last words, "died and stank," have the initial letters of "*Sarah Esther bat Yehudith, vay metah*—Sarah Esther bat Yehudit woe has died." May God protect us!

Rabbi Nachman told his followers that whenever they experienced a nocturnal emission, they should immediately immerse in a mikvah. As a result of this nocturnal pollution, whatever damage was done, was done. However, before a permanent impression is made, one should immerse and purify oneself.

Rabbi Nachman warned that one should not be frightened by this at all. Fear, worry, and depression are very harmful as far as this is concerned. This is especially true now that he has revealed the Ten Psalms that have the specific power to rectify this sin.

The Ten Psalms are Psalms 16, 32, 41, 42, 59, 77, 90, 105, 137, and 150, as discussed in our printed works.* If a person recites these ten psalms on the day that he has had a nocturnal emission, his sin is rectified, and he need not have any further concern.

Rabbi Nachman laughed at Chasidim and God-fearing men who were terrified whenever they had an untoward thought, lest they experience a nocturnal pollution. However, the fear itself can often bring that which they wished to avoid. He therefore mocked this.

His main teaching was that a person not be afraid or terrified by this. One should not think about it at all. One should be like a mighty warrior, standing up against one's desires, utterly fearless, and not thinking of them at all. Then, "God will do what is good in His eyes" (I Samuel 3:18), as He desires.

---

our printed works. See *Likutey Moharan* B 92; *Sichoth HaRan* 141. The Ten Psalms are published separately as *Tikkun HaKelali* (The General Rectification). See Bibliography.

In his discussion, Rabbi Nachman hinted that this was the blemish of King David and Bathsheva... However, he did not explain this very clearly.

However, a man must strengthen himself in joy at all times, and not let anything depress him, no matter what happens. If he is strong in his resolve, he will not be afraid at all, and will not dwell upon such thoughts. He will travel in his simple way with joy, and he will overcome everything in peace.

It is impossible to put such words into writing. However, "a prudent man will follow the right path" (Proverbs 14:15).

*

On the Sabbath of Chanukah he told a story that was partially forgotten. It involved the son of a king who was far away from his father, and yearned very much. He received a letter from his father, and was very happy because of it. He yearned very much at least to reach out a hand, and if a hand were extended, he would hug it and kiss it.

The son then made up his mind that the letter was the handwriting of the king himself. Therefore, it is the "hand" of the king. (All of this was not written exactly, since it was not recorded at the time it was said.)

Finished and completed, praise to God Creator of the Universe. Blessed is "He who gives power to the faint, and who increases the strength of one who has no energy" (Isaiah 40:29).

6   The Thief*

Once there was a poor man who sat in the synagogue and studied Torah. An astrologer* came to the city, and the entire populace ran to him. The poor man, however, did not go. When his wife came to the synagogue, she did not find anyone there other than her husband, since everyone else had gone to the astrologer. She began screaming at him, "You are a lazy, hapless beggar! Why don't you go to the astrologer?"

He did not want to go, but his wife kept pressing him until he had no choice. When he finally got to the astrologer, the astrologer told him that it was his destiny to be a thief.

The man returned to the synagogue, to his Torah study. His wife came to him and asked, "What did he tell you?"

"He told me that I am a poor man and I will remain a poor man," replied her husband.

That night, he came home and ate a piece of bread as his main meal. During the meal, he began to laugh. His wife asked him, "Why are you laughing? You must know something that you're not telling me."

"No," he replied. "He did not tell me anything. I'm just laughing for the fun of it."

He continued eating, and suddenly, he laughed again. When his wife asked him why, he replied to her as before. Then, all of a sudden, he began to roar with laughter. She said to him, "Now I'm sure that you know something." He replied, "Yes, it's true. The astrologer told me that it is my destiny to be a thief."

The Thief. The collection of the following stories ("The Thief" through "Trust in God") is not in *Sippurey Maasioth*, but in *Maasioth U'Meshalim*, in *Kokhavay Or*, beginning on page 14. They were originally found in a notebook of Rabbi Naftali, one of Rabbi Nachman's close disciples (ibid., p. 13). These stories are only in Hebrew, with some Yiddish phrases thrown in.

astrologer. *Rosh bit* in Yiddish.

103

His wife replied, "I do not want you to be a thief. It is better that we remain poor. Let us accept what God gives us. Don't become a thief."

When the Sabbath came, they had everything that they needed. They had bread, and everything else. When they sat down to eat, they had four or five girls, and the girls grabbed the bread, since there was not enough for all of them. The wife said, "Lord of the Universe. It is so disgusting to me to be so poor!" Addressing her husband, she said, "I would rather have you be a thief, so that we should not be so poor!" The poor man did not have any choice but to obey her.* He wanted to, he did not want to, but he went all the same. The Rebbe used this expression several times when he told this story.

The husband went out to steal. His first victim was the wealthiest man in town. When he got there, he found the watchmen sleeping, and no one asked him a thing. He went to the store, and found the lock open, since this was his destiny. When he went to the strongbox, it was also unlocked. He took four or five rubles, just enough to support himself, and brought them to his wife.

"I did as you asked," he said. "This should be enough to support us. But I don't want to have to steal again!"

"I agree with you completely," she replied. "I also don't want you ever to steal again. We only had to do it this time, since things were so tight."

But then, once again, an occasion arose when she screamed at him, "Beggar! Hapless fool! You were in the store already? Why didn't you take enough to buy me a coat."*

The man had to go steal again. When he got there, he found another thief. "Who are you?" he asked.

"A thief," replied the other. "Who are you?"

"Also a thief," replied the poor man. "Let's be partners in crime. This is my destiny, and I know that I will be successful."

They agreed. However, the poor man began to think, "If we steal here, we will impoverish our victim. When I was alone, I would only

---

to obey her. In parentheses in Yiddish, "Whether he wanted to go or not, he went anyway."

coat. *Yupa.* See the story of "The Sophisticate and the Simpleton" in *The Lost Princess.*

steal enough for a coat for my wife. But now we will steal very much, and the victim will remain without anything."

"Why should we make a fellow Jew suffer a loss?" he said to the other. "Better let us steal from a gentile."

They agreed to this, and decided to steal from the king (who lived in that city). The poor man was sure that he would be successful, since that was his destiny.

The thief said, "The best thing to steal would be the outfit the king wore at his coronation. This is so valuable that it would suffice us for many generations. I know where these clothes are kept."

The poor man agreed. He was sure that he would be able to steal them, since this was his destiny.

They went to the palace, and went from one room to another and finally came to the garments. The garments were very precious, and this is what they took.

They then began to argue. There was one large garment and one small garment. The thief said that since he was the one who knew about them, he should get the larger one. The poor man, on the other hand, said that he deserved it, since he was the man of destiny, and it was because of destiny that the theft was successful.

"Let us take our dispute to the king," declared the poor man.

"How could you possibly do that?" asked the thief.

"It does not matter," said the poor man. "I will go and ask him."

"If you do that," said the thief, "and actually ask the king, then I will give you the large garment of my own accord."

The thief went with him to the king. Reclining next to the king was a man who told the king stories to put him to sleep. The two of them took the bed with the king sleeping on it, and carried it to another room. When the king woke up, he thought that he was in his usual place.

The poor man began to tell the king the story of the two thieves. When he ended, he asked the king, "Who deserves the larger garment?"

The king became very angry. "Why are you asking me such a simple question?" he said. "It obviously should go to the poor man, since it is because of his destiny that the theft was successful. Now, you'd better tell me a story!"

The poor man told him a story, and the king fell asleep. They then carried the bed back to its original room.

In the morning, it was discovered that the king's royal garments had been stolen. The king remembered that the one reclining near him had asked who should get the larger garment. The regular story teller was therefore beaten, but he said that he knew nothing about it. They beat and tortured him very much, but he kept on insisting that he did not know anything about the theft.

The king sent for the archbishop* to ask him about these strange happenings, and if it was possible that the storyteller really was not the thief. The archbishop said that it was possible that he was ignorant of the crime. He also said that the king was foolish to say that the larger garment belonged to the poor man. The king became very angry with the archbishop, and wanted to punish him, but he could do nothing.

Meanwhile, the thieves were being sought, but they could not be found. Finally, the king ordered that an announcement be made that whoever had perpetrated the theft should come out, and he would not be harmed. The king felt that he had to satisfy his curiosity as to how the garments were stolen. There were many people around him talking about the case.

Finally the poor man came, and asked the people what they were speaking about. When they told him, he said, "What's the fuss? Let the one who stole return it."

The people rebuked him. When he asked a second time, they rebuked him again. "Beggar! You deserve to be killed. It is being said that you know something about the theft."

"Yes," replied the poor man, "I know who the thief is."

"If you know, then you must tell," they said.

"I will tell," he replied.

The poor man came to the king, and said, "I know who the thief is."

"I would very much like to see the thief," replied the king.

"I am he!" said the poor man.

The king kissed him and asked, "How did you do it?"

---

archbishop. Leader of priests, called *archriga.*

The poor man told him the entire story. They caught the other thief, and he had to return the second garment which he had.

The king then said to the poor man, "I would like you to play a similar trick on the archbishop, since I am very angry with him."

The poor man said, "Give me a set of vestments like the archbishop wears during his service. I will also need a large number of turtles* captured for me. Besides that, I will need many candles."

The poor man put on the vestments, and attached a candle to each turtle. He then stood at the altar, and began to scream. Everyone gathered, and the archbishop came with them. The archbishop was very frightened, since he saw fires and heard a voice crying out, but did not know what it was.

The poor man said to the archbishop, "I have come for you. I want to bring you into paradise immediately."

The archbishop fell on his face.

"Before I take you to paradise," said the poor man, "I must first bring you through purgatory for a short time. Then I will bring you to paradise. First you must get into my sack."

When the archbishop was in the sack, the poor man carried him to the king. The sack was hung up in the palace courtyard, and the king was informed. People came and saw the sack hanging with someone obviously inside it, and they began to throw stones at it. The archbishop was severely wounded and all his teeth were broken. The archbishop did not know what was happening; was this purgatory as he had been told, or was it all a trick?

After he had been well beaten, the king gave orders to cut him down. The sack was cut down and opened, and the archbishop left in humiliation.*

turtles. *Rakis.*

humiliation. In another version, "In the end, he was hung, since 'the end of a thief is hanging.' While he was being brought, the Evil One walked alongside with a sack of shoes, and he said, 'I wore out all these shoes until I finally brought you to this.'

7 Faith

There was once a poor man who earned a living by digging clay and selling it. Once, while digging clay, he discovered a precious stone which was obviously worth a great deal. Since he had no idea of its worth, he took it to an expert to tell him its value.

The expert answered, "No one here will be able to afford such a stone. Go to London, the capital, and there you will be able to sell it."

The man was so poor that he could not afford to make the journey. He sold everything he had, and went from house to house, collecting funds for the trip. Finally he had enough to take him as far as the sea.

He then wanted to board a ship, but he did not have any money. He went to a ship's captain and showed him the jewel. The captain immediately welcomed him aboard the ship with great honor, assuming that he was a very trustworthy person. He gave the poor man a special first class cabin, and treated him like a wealthy personage.

The poor man's cabin had a view of the sea, and he sat there, constantly looking at the diamond and rejoicing. He was especially particular to do this during his meals, since eating in such good spirits is highly beneficial for the digestion.

Then one day, he sat down to eat, with the diamond lying in front of him on the table where he could enjoy it. Sitting there, he dozed off. Meanwhile, the mess boy came and cleared the table, shaking the tablecloth with its crumbs and the diamond into the sea. When he woke up and realized what had happened, he almost went mad with grief. Besides, the captain was a ruthless man who would not hesitate to kill him for his fare.

Having no other choice, he continued to act happy, as if nothing had happened. The captain would usually speak to him a few hours every day, and on this day, he put himself in good spirits, so that the captain was not aware that anything was wrong.

The captain said to him, "I want to buy a large quantity of wheat and I will be able to sell it in London for a huge profit. But I am afraid that I will be accused of stealing from the king's treasury. Therefore, I will arrange for the wheat to be bought in your name. I will pay you well for your trouble."

The poor man agreed. But as soon as they arrived in London, the captain died. The entire shipload of wheat was in the poor man's name, and it was worth many times as much as the diamond.

Rabbi Nachman concluded, "The diamond did not belong to the poor man, and the proof is that he did not keep it. The wheat, however, did belong to him, and the proof is that he kept it. But he got what he deserved only because he *remained* happy."

8 Kaptzin Pasha

Once there was a court Jew who was very much favored by the Turkish Sultan, more than any of the other ministers of state. The Sultan was very fond of him, more than anyone else in his government. Every day, the Sultan would invite him to his palace to spend time with him.

The other royal ministers grew jealous of him, and devised plots to denounce him to the Sultan and destroy him.

Among the ministers, there was a pasha named Kaptzin Pasha, who hated this Jew more than anyone else in the government. When he was with the court Jew, he behaved like a close friend. But every day he would devise plots to denounce the Jew before the Sultan.

Once the Pasha came to the Jew and began to speak to him. He maliciously told him, "I was with the Sultan, and I heard him say that he is very fond of you. There is, however, one thing that bothers him. Whenever you come to him and speak with him, he can't stand your bad breath. Since he does not want to avoid you, this troubles him very much. My advice is that when you come to the Sultan you should place a perfumed handkerchief over your mouth. This will cover up your bad breath, so that it will not disturb the Sultan."

In his innocence, the Jew believed him, and agreed to follow his advice.

The Pasha then went to the Sultan and told him that he had heard the Jew say that he suffers very much since whenever he speaks to the Sultan, he has to smell the Sultan's bad breath. "Therefore," said the Pasha, "Whenever the Jew comes to you, he will place a perfumed handkerchief over his mouth, so that he will not smell your breath. And if you don't believe me, this is proof. Tomorrow when the Jew comes, he will have a handkerchief over his mouth."

When the Sultan heard this, he became very angry. He said, "I will see if you are telling the truth! If it is true, I will destroy that Jew!"

111

The next day, when the Jew came to the Sultan, he placed the hand-kerchief over his mouth, just as the Pasha had advised him, since he had believed him. When the Sultan saw that, he understood that the Pasha had been telling the truth. He immediately wrote a note saying, "When the bearer of this note arrives, immediately throw him into the furnace where all those who are sentenced to death are cast." The Sultan then sealed the letter with his signet, and said to the Jew, "Do me a favor and personally deliver this note to the man whose address is written on the envelope."

The Jew took the letter and promised the Sultan that he would do as he requested, not knowing what was written in the letter.

The court Jew was very diligent to keep the commandment to cir-cumcise Jewish children. Whenever he was honored to perform a cir-cumcision,* he would not pay attention to any obstacle, since this commandment was very precious to him.

On that very day, when he was supposed to deliver the Sultan's letter to the place it was sent, God arranged to save His good friend. He made it happen that a man came from a village, and honored the court Jew to travel with him to the village to circumcise his son. The custom of the court Jew was not to avoid performing this precept, no matter what the circumstances. He began to think, "What will I do to fulfill the Sultan's request that I deliver the letter?"

God then arranged that he should meet Kaptzin Pasha. The court Jew told the Pasha that he had been with the Sultan, and that the Sultan had given him a letter to deliver. But now God had arranged that he could perform a circumcision, and his custom was not to set aside this commandment for any reason whatever. "Therefore," he said, "I am asking you to do me a favor. Please, if you would, take the letter, and deliver it there."

The Pasha was very happy at the turn of events, since now he would also be able to denounce the Jew for not delivering the letter as

---

to perform a circumcision. *Chitukh* in Hebrew. This is the cutting off of the foreskin. Often, another person would be honored to pull it back (*periyah*). In those times, it was a cus-tom to give honor to people by having them perform these ceremonies.

the Sultan had ordered. He immediately took the letter and delivered it to the one to whom it was addressed. The recipient was the executioner in charge of burning those who had been sentenced to death by the Sultan. He immediately grabbed the Pasha and threw him into the furnace. He was burned as he had been judged by God, and was thus punished "measure for measure."*

The Jew, meanwhile, did not know anything about this, and the next day he appeared before the Sultan as if nothing had happened. When the Sultan saw him, he was very surprised. "Didn't you deliver the letter that I gave you?" he asked.

The Jew replied, "Your Majesty, I gave the letter to Kaptzin Pasha to deliver. God gave me the opportunity to perform a circumcision, and my custom is not to pass over this opportunity whenever it presents itself."

The Sultan then understood that there was a reason that the Pasha had been burned, and that it was because he had slandered the Jew. The Sultan asked him, "How come you hold a perfumed handkerchief over your mouth when you speak to me?"

"The Pasha advised me to," replied the Jew. "He told me that he heard you saying that you couldn't stand my bad breath."

The Sultan then told him how the Pasha had slandered the Jew. He said, "The Pasha said that you couldn't stand my bad breath, and that you were putting the perfumed handkerchief over your mouth to avoid smelling it."

The Sultan then revealed to the Jew the contents of the letter. He said, "Now I know that God has power over the world, and He saved His friend from all evil. What the Pasha wanted to do to you was done to him. He was paid back as he deserved."

The Jew was now all the more esteemed by the Sultan, more so than any of his ministers of state. He was very highly esteemed and dear to him.

---

measure for measure. *Middah ke-neged middah.* The concept that God always makes the punishment fit the crime; it is found in many places in the Talmud (see *Sotah* 9b).

9 Simplicity

God wins battles merely because of the simple folk who recite psalms with simplicity, and not through those who use sophisticated means.

A king once went hunting,* and he traveled like a simple man, so that he would have freedom of movement. Suddenly a heavy rain fell, literally like a flood. The ministers scattered in all directions, and the king was in great danger. He searched until he found the house of a villager. The villager invited the king in and offered him some groats.* He lit the stove, and let the king sleep on the pallet.*

This was very sweet and pleasant for the king. He was so tired and exhausted that it seemed as if he had never had such a pleasurable experience.

Meanwhile, the royal ministers sought the king, until they found him in this house, where they saw the king sleeping. They wanted him to return to the palace with them.

"You did not even attempt to rescue me," said the king. "Each one of you ran to save himself. But this man rescued me. Here I had the sweetest experience. Therefore, he will bring me back in his wagon, in these clothes, and he will sit with me on my throne."

Rabbi Nachman concluded by saying that it is said that before the Messiah comes, there will be flood. (People will be flooded with atheism.)

hunting. *Navlavi.*
groats. *Graetz.*
pallet. *Pieklik.*

It will not be a flood of water, but of immorality.* It will cover all the high mountains,* even in the Holy Land, where the original flood did not reach.* But this time, it will come with such strength that the water will splash over the land. This means that it will have an effect even in virtuous hearts.

There will be no way to combat this with sophistication. All the royal ministers will be scattered, and the entire kingdom will not be firm on its foundation. The only ones who will uphold it will be the simple Jews who recite Psalms in simplicity. Therefore, when the Messiah comes, they will be the ones to place the crown on his head.

immorality. The abbrevation here is *Mem Zayin,* which can denote *mayim zedim, makhshavoth zaroth.*

cover all the high mountains. Genesis 7:21.

Holy Land... There is an opinion in the Talmud that the flood did not cover the Land of Israel (*Zevachim* 113b).

10   Verda

Once a man was traveling with his teamster (to Berlin and other large cities). The man went aside to attend his needs, and the driver, whose name was Ivan, remained with the coach in the middle of the street. A soldier came along and asked, "Why is it standing there? Who is it?" In German, "Who is it" is *wer da*, or as pronounced in Yiddish, Verda.

The driver thought that the soldier was asking his name, so he replied, "Ivan."

The soldier gave him a blow to the head. "Verda!" he demanded.

"Ivan!" screamed the driver.

The soldier hit him again, and shouted "Verda!"

Finally, the soldier took him and the wagon to a side street. When the man came back, he looked around until he found his coach. He said to the driver, "Ivan..."

The driver was terrified. "Don't call me Ivan!" he said. "Call me Verda."

When they finally left the city, he said, "Now you can call me Ivan. There my name was Verda, but here my name is Ivan."

Rabbi Nachman concluded by saying, "By me it is Verda." (That is, "who is it.") One knows his lowly status. Also when the body (Ivan) is purified, it is called, "who" and "what." But when people leave me, then they become Ivan again, since the physical remains physical.

11   The Bitter Herb

Once a Jew and a German gentile were traveling as hoboes together. The Jew told the German to make believe that he was a Jew (since their language was similar), and the Jews would have pity on him. Since Passover was approaching, he taught him how to act (when he is invited to a Seder). He told him that at every Seder,* Kiddush* is made, and the hands are washed. However, he forgot to tell him about the bitter herb.

He was invited to a house, and being very hungry from all day, looked forward to the fine foods that had been described by the Jew. However, first they gave him a piece of celery* dipped in salt water, and other things served at the Seder. They then began to recite the Haggadah* and he sat there longing for the meal. When the matzah was served, he was very happy.

Then they gave him a piece of horseradish for the bitter herb.* It was bitter to taste, and he thought that this was the entire meal. He ran from the house, bitter and hungry, saying to himself, "Cursed Jews! After all that ceremony, that's all they serve to eat!" He went to the synagogue and fell asleep.

After a while, the Jew arrived, happy and full from a good meal. "How was your Seder?" he asked.

The other told him what had happened.

"Stupid German!" replied the Jew. "If you had waited just a little longer, you would have had a fine meal, as I had."

Seder. The traditional Passover night feast.

Kiddush. The prayer over wine that begins the Seder.

celery. *Karpas.* Celery is dipped in salt water and eaten at the very beginning of the Seder, before the Haggadah (story of the Exodus) is recited.

Haggadah. The story of the exodus from Egypt.

bitter herb. It is eaten just before the meal.

The same is true when one wants to come close to God. After all the effort to begin, one is given a little bitterness. This bitterness is needed to purify the body. But the person might think that this bitterness is all there is to serving God, so he runs away from it. But if he waited a short while, and allowed his body to be purified, then he would feel every joy and delight in the world in his closeness to God.

12　The Treasure

A man once dreamed that there was a great treasure under a bridge in Vienna. He traveled to Vienna and stood near the bridge, trying to figure out what to do. He did not dare search for the treasure by day, because of the many people who were there.

An officer passed by and asked, "What are you doing, standing here and contemplating?" The man decided that it would be best to tell the whole story and ask for help, hoping that the officer would share the treasure with him. He told the officer the entire story.

The officer replied, "A Jew is concerned only with dreams! I also had a dream, and I also saw a treasure. It was in a small house, under the cellar."

In relating his dream, the officer accurately described the man's city and house. He rushed home, dug under his cellar, and found the treasure. He said, "Now I know that I had the treasure all along. But in order to find it, I had to travel to Vienna."

The same is true in serving God. Each person has the treasure, but in order to find it, he must travel to the tzaddik.

13   The Turkey Prince

A royal prince once became mad and thought that he was a turkey. He felt compelled to sit naked under the table, pecking at bones and pieces of bread like a turkey. The royal physicians all gave up hope of ever curing him of this madness, and the king suffered tremendous grief.

A sage then came and said, "I will undertake to cure him."

The sage undressed and sat naked under the table next to the prince, picking crumbs and bones. "Who are you?" asked the prince. "What are you doing here?"

"And you?" replied the sage. "What are you doing here?"

"I am a turkey," said the prince.

"I am also a turkey," answered the sage.

They sat together like this for some time, until they became good friends. One day, the sage signalled the king's servants to throw him shirts. He said to the prince, "What makes you think that a turkey can't wear a shirt? You can wear a shirt and still be a turkey." With that, the two of them put on shirts.

After a while, he signalled them again, and they threw him a pair of pants. Just as before, he said, "What makes you think that you can't be a turkey if you wear pants?"

The sage continued in this manner until they were both completely dressed. Then he signalled again, and they were given regular food from the table. Again the sage said, "What makes you think that you will stop being a turkey if you eat good food? You can eat whatever you want and still be a turkey!" They both ate the food.

Finally, the sage said, "What makes you think a turkey must sit under the table? Even a turkey can sit at the table."

The sage continued in this manner until the prince was completely cured.

14   The Tainted Grain

A king once told his prime minister, who was also his good friend, "I see in the stars that whoever eats any grain that grows this year will go mad.* What is your advice?"

The prime minister replied, "We must put aside enough grain so that we will not have to eat from this year's harvest."

The king objected, "But then we will be the only ones who will be sane. Everyone else will be mad. Therefore, they will think that we are the mad ones. It is impossible for us to put aside enough grain for everyone. Therefore, we too must eat this year's grain. But we will make a mark on our foreheads, so that at least we will know that we are mad. I will look at your forehead, and you will look at mine, and when we see this sign, we will know that we are both mad."

---

mad. There are fungi of the ergot family that attack grain and can cause hallucinations and other bizarre experiences when ingested. These fungi contain substances very similar to LSD.

15 The Deer

Once a king was pursuing a deer, but he could not catch it. The royal ministers caught up with him and said, "Your Majesty, let's go back."

"I must capture the deer," replied the king. "But whoever wishes to go back can go back."

16   The Bird

There was once a king who was a great astrologer. One year he saw in the stars that if the wheat was not harvested before a certain time, all the wheat would be ruined. He saw that there was not much time.

He came up with the idea that he would give the harvesters every possible pleasure and all their needs, so that they would have a clear mind to work day and night. Then they would finish the harvest before the deadline.

However, the workers took what the king sent them, and they enjoyed themselves so much that they forgot to work on the harvest. The time came, and the wheat was not harvested, so that it became completely ruined.

The people did not know what to do. They realized that the king would be terribly angry with them.

A sage gave them an idea. The king was very fond of a certain type of bird. If they could bring him such a bird, he would have so much pleasure from it, he would forgive everything. However, it was very difficult to capture this bird, since it lived very high up. They did not have a ladder, and there was no time to get one.

The sage once again gave them an idea. Since they were many men, one would be able to stand on the shoulders of the other, making a human ladder to reach the bird.

They liked the idea, but began to argue, since each one wanted to be on top. They wasted time arguing, until the bird flew away. The king then remained angry at them for neglecting to harvest the wheat on time.

The idea is that God created man, and gave him every pleasure, all so that he should "cut the grain" before he is harmed through blemishing the covenant of Abraham (*pegam ha-b'rith*). People would then be able to serve God with a clear mind. But they neglected it through their enjoyment, until they forgot the grain, and let their minds be ruined. Nevertheless, there was still hope through the bird, who is the tzaddik, since through him everything could be forgiven. But then there was arguing and strife, since each one wanted to be on top. They were thus kept from binding themselves to the tzaddik.

17   Trust in God*

There was once a king who said to himself, "Who can have fewer worries than I have? I have everything good and I am a king and a ruler."

He went to investigate this. He walked around at night, standing behind the houses, to listen and determine what people were saying. He heard each one's worries, and how things were not going well in their business. At one person's house, he heard that the person had troubles, and had to obtain an audience with the king. In this way, he heard each one's complaints.

Then he saw a very low house, that was sunken in the ground, so that its windows were literally at ground level. Its roof was fallen and broken. Inside he saw a man sitting and playing his fiddle, but he had to listen very well to hear the sound. The man was very happy. He had a plate and drink in front of him. The drink was wine, and he had other food before him. The man appeared very happy, full of joy, without any worries.

The king went into the house, and asked how the man was getting along. The man replied. The king saw the pot, the wine and the food in front of the man, and saw the joy on the man's face. The man gave the king some wine, and drank to the king. Out of love, the king also drank.

Trust in God. This story was first printed in Jerusalem around 1905 by Rabbi Tzvi Dov ben Avraham of Berdichev. It was printed in both Hebrew and Yiddish. It seems that it was either preserved in manuscript or told orally in Uman.

At the beginning of the story, it states that Rabbi Nachman told this story on 4 Elul, 5566 (August 18, 1806). Shortly before this (July 27), Rabbi Nachman had spoken of how one can accept all suffering with love and faith (*Likutey Moharan*, New Sayings, at end of volume, p. 4; *Shevachay Moharan* 35a 124; *Likutey Halakhoth*, Geviyath Chov 4:10).

This story was also told just about a month after the story of "The Lost Princess" (see *The Lost Princess*), which was told on July 25, 1806.

The king then lay down to sleep. The king saw that he was totally happy, without any worries whatever.

In the morning the king got up, and the man also got up and accompanied the king.

"Where do you get all this?" asked the king.

"I am a repairman," replied the man. "I can fix anything that is broken. I can't make anything, but I can fix things. I go out in the morning, and I fix things. When I have five or six gulden, I buy myself food and drink."

When the king heard this, he said to himself, "I will ruin him."

The king returned home, and issued a decree that if anyone has anything broken, he should not give it to anyone to fix. He must either fix it himself, or buy something new.

The next morning, the fixer went out, and looked for things to repair. He was told that the king had issued a decree that nothing be given to others to fix. This was bad for him, but he had trust in God.

He walked a while, and saw a wealthy man cutting wood. "Why are you cutting the wood yourself?" asked the fixer. "Isn't it beneath your dignity?"

"I tried to find someone to cut the wood for me," replied the rich man, "but I couldn't find anyone. I had no choice but to cut it myself."

"Let me," replied the fixer. "I will cut the wood for you."

He cut the wood, and the rich man gave him a gulden. He saw that this was a good way to earn money, so he went to cut more wood, until he had earned six gulden. He took the money and bought himself his meal. The meal was a feast and he was very happy.

The king went out again that night, and stood outside the fixer's window to see what had happened. He saw the fixer sitting with food and drink in front of him, very happy. The king came in, and saw the same as the previous time. They then went to sleep as they had done previously, and in the morning the man got up and accompanied the king.

"Where did you get your food?" asked the king. "How did you earn money for it?"

"My usual work is to repair things," replied the fixer. "But the king made a law that nothing can be given to another to be fixed. So I went and chopped wood until I got enough money for what I needed."

After leaving the fixer, the king issued a decree that no one should hire anyone to cut wood.

When the man heard this, he was upset, since he had no money. But still, he trusted in God. He walked a while, and saw a man cleaning out his stable. "Who are you to be cleaning out a stable?" he asked.

"I looked all over," replied the other, "and I couldn't find anyone to do it for me. Therefore, I had to do it myself."

"Let me," replied the fixer. "I will clean it out for you."

When he was finished the man gave him two gulden. He cleaned out a few more stables, and earned himself the six gulden that he needed. He bought his entire meal, and returned home. The meal was for him a feast, and he was very happy.

The king went out again to see what had happened, and again saw him happy. The king came in, spent the night, and in the morning, the fixer accompanied the king. The king asked him how he got the money, and he explained what he had done. The king then issued a decree that no one may be hired to clean out barns or stables.

That morning, the fixer went out to clean stables, but he was told that the king had made a law that no one be hired to do such work. Not having any choice, the fixer went to the recruiting officer and joined the national guard. Some soldiers are drafted, but others volunteer for pay.

The fixer hired himself out as a soldier, and made a condition with the recruiting officer that he would only join temporarily, and that he would be paid every morning. He immediately put on his uniform, and put his sword at his side. At night, he took off his uniform, and with his pay, he bought himself his meal and went home. The meal was a feast for him, and he was very happy.

The king went out to see what had happened. He saw that everything was set before the fixer, and that he was very happy. He entered the house, and spent the night with him as before. The king then asked him how he was getting along, and the fixer told him the whole story. The king called the officer and told him that he should not lift a finger to pay any of the men from the treasury that morning.

When the fixer reported for duty, he asked the officer for his pay for the day. When the officer would not pay him, he said, "But we made an agreement that you would pay me every day."

"True," replied the officer, "but the king decreed that no one get paid today."

The fixer pleaded and argued, but to no avail. "I'll pay you tomorrow for two days," said the officer. "But today it is impossible to pay you."

The fixer devised a plan. He removed the blade from his sword, and replaced it with a wooden blade, so that no one could tell the difference. He then pawned the sword blade and bought his meal as usual. The meal was a feast.

The king came back again, and saw the fixer completely happy. He came to visit and spent the night, and asked him how things were doing. The fixer told him the whole story, how he had removed the sword blade from the handle, and had pawned it to buy his meal. "When I get paid today," he finished, "I will redeem the blade and fix it. No one will know the difference. I can fix anything! The king will have lost nothing."

When the king returned to his palace, he summoned the officer in charge. He said, "I have a criminal who was sentenced to death. Call this fixer whom you recruited as a mercenary, and give him orders to cut off this criminal's head."

The officer went and summoned the fixer. The king gave orders that all the officers should see this joke. He told them that one of his soldiers had replaced the blade of his sword with a wooden substitute.

When the fixer came before the king, he fell on the ground before the king, and pleaded, "Your Majesty. Why did you summon me?"

"To decapitate a criminal," replied the king.

The fixer begged and pleaded. "But I have never killed a man," he said. "Please! Get someone else to do it."

"That's just why I'm ordering you to do it," replied the king.

"Is the case really that clear?" asked the fixer. "Maybe the case is not clear. Maybe he doesn't deserve to die. I never killed a man in my life. How can I now kill someone who might not even deserve to die?"

"There is no question whatsoever that he deserves to die," replied the king. "The verdict is unanimous. And you must be the one to carry out the sentence and execute him."

The fixer saw that he would not be able to dissuade the king. He looked up toward heaven and said, "God Almighty. I never killed a person in my life. If this man does not deserve to die, let the blade of my sword turn to wood."

With that, he drew his sword, and everyone saw that the blade was a piece of wood. All those present had a good laugh. The king saw what a fine man the fixer was, and he let him go home in peace.

Bibliography

Adir BaMarom. Important work on Kabbalistic thought by Rabbi Moshe Chaim Luzzatto (1707–1746), first published in Warsaw, 1882. The author was considered one of the most important of all Kabbalistic thinkers, and is best known for his *Mesillath Yesharim (Path of the Upright)*.

Adney Kesef. Biblical commentary by Rabbi Yosef (ben Abba Mari) ibn Caspi (1279–1340), first published from manuscript by Yitchak Last, London, 1911. The author was a leading Jewish thinker in Spain.

Alim LeTerufah. Collection of letters by Rabbi Nathan (ben Naftali Hertz) Sternhartz of Nemirov (1780–1844), first published in Berdichev, 1896, and with editions in Jerusalem, 1911. A more complete edition was published by Rabbi Aaron Leib Tziegelman in Jerusalem, 1930. We have used the Jerusalem, 1968, edition. Rabbi Nathan was the foremost disciple of Rabbi Nachman, and publisher of many of his works, including the Stories. Translated into English as *Eternally Yours: The Collected Letters of Reb Noson of Breslov.* Published by the Breslov Research Institute in 1993.

Anaf Yosef. Commentary on *Eyn Yaakov* (q.v.), by Rabbi Chanokh Zundel ben Yosef (died 1867), first published together with his other commentary, *Etz Yosef,* in the Vilna, 1883, edition of *Eyn Yaakov.* The author, who lived in Bialystok, Poland, wrote commentaries on numerous Midrashim.

Arba Meyoth Shekel Kesef. Important work on the Kabbalah of the Ari (Rabbi Yitzchak Luria, 1534–1572), by Rabbi Chaim Vital (1542–1620), first published in Koretz, 1804. We have used the Cracow, 1886, edition. See *Etz Chaim.*

Arukh. One of the earliest and most popular dictionaries of the Talmud (q.v.) by Rabbi Nathan (ben Yechiel) of Rome (1035–1106), first printed in Rome, 1472.

The author was a colleague of Rabbenu Gershom, leader of Ashkenazic Jewry, and corresponded with Rashi (q.v.).

Avanehah Barzel. Stories and teachings of Rabbi Nachman and his disciples, collected by Rabbi Shmuel Horowitz (1903–1973), first printed in Jerusalem, 1935. We have used the Jerusalem, 1972, edition, printed together with *Kokhavey Or* (q.v.). The author was an important Breslover leader in Jerusalem.

Avkath Rokhel. Ethical and escatological work by Rabbi Makhir, first printed in Constantinople, 1516.

Avodath HaKodesh. Important Kabbalistic work by Rabbi Meir ibn Gabbai (born 1480), first published in Venice, 1567. Born in Spain, the author lived in Egypt and Safed after the expulsion.

Avoth deRabbi Nathan. A running commentary on *Avoth,* by the Babylonian sage, Rabbi Nathan (circa 210 CE). It is printed in all editions of the Talmud. We follow the paragraphing of the Vilna, 1883, Romm edition of the Talmud.

Bahir. An important ancient Kabbalistic work, attributed to the school of Rabbi Nechunia ben Hakana (circa 80 CE), first printed in Amsterdam, 1651. An English translation by Rabbi Aryeh Kaplan was published by Weiser (York, Maine, 1979).

BaMidbar Rabbah. Part of the *Midrash Rabbah* (q.v.) dealing with the Book of Numbers.

Batey Midrashoth. A collection of ancient Midrashim and similar material from manuscript by Rabbi Shlomo Aaron Wertheimer (1866–1935), first published in Jerusalem, 1893–1897, and with additions, Jerusalem, 1950.

Belbey HaNachal. Commentary on *Likutey Moharan* (q.v.), by Rabbi Barukh Ephraim (ben Yitzchak), first printed together with *Parparoth LeChokhman* (q.v.) in Lvov (Lemberg), 1876. It was later printed with *Likutey Moharan,* New York, 1966.

Bereshith Rabbah. The section of the *Midrash Rabbah* (q.v.) dealing with the Book of Genesis. It is a commentary on the Scripture, based on Talmudic material.

Beth Halevi. Commentary on the Torah (two volumes) by Rabbi Yoseph Dov (ben Rabbi Yitzchak Zev) Halevi Soloveitchik. Rabbi Yoseph Dov was a descendant of Rabbi Chaim of Volozshin, and a leading rabbinical authority in Lithuania. The first edition was printed in Vilna.

Biur HaLikutim. Commentary on *Likutey Moharan* (q.v.) by Rabbi Avraham (Chazan HaLevi) ben Reb Nachman of Tulchin (1849–1917), printed in part in Jerusalem, 1908, and in greater part, B'nei B'rak, 1967.

Burstyn, Rabbi Nachman. Oral teachings, by a leading figure in Breslov in Jerusalem.

Butril, Rabbi Moshe. Commentary on *Sefer Yetzirah* (q.v.) written in 1409, and first printed in the Mantua, 1562, edition of *Sefer Yetzirah.* The author was an important Kabbalist and quotes a number of sources no longer in existence.

Chayay Moharan. Important biographical work on Rabbi Nachman, by his chief disciple, Rabbi Nathan of Nemerov (see *Alim LeTerufah*), printed with notes by Rabbi Nachman of Tcherin, Lemberg, 1874. We have used the Jerusalem, 1962, edition. Translated into English as *Tzaddik: A Portrait of Rebbe Nachman.* Published by the Breslov Research Institute in 1987.

Chayay Nefesh. Kabbalistic discussion of Breslover principles, by Rabbi Gedalia Aaron (ben Eleazar Mordechai) Koenig (1921–1980), published in Tel Aviv, 1968.

Chokhmah U'Tevunah. Kabbalistic commentary on the Stories by Rabbi Avraham ben Nachman of Tulchin, first published in B'nei B'rak, 1962.

Choshen Mishpat. Fourth section of the *Shulchan Arukh* (q.v.) dealing with judicial law.

Daath Chokhmah. Penetrating Kabbalistic work by Rabbi Moshe Chaim Luzzatto (see *Adir BaMarom*), first printed as part of *Pith'chey Chokhmah VeDaath*, Warsaw, 1884. Reprinted with *Klach Pith'chey Chokhmah*, Jerusalem, 1961.

Dan Yadin. Commentary on *Karnayim* (q.v.) by Rabbi Shimshon (ben Pesach) Ostropoli (died 1648), first published in Zolkiev, 1709. We have used the Amsterdam, 1765 edition, reprinted in B'nei B'rak, 1971. The author was the leading Kabbalist in Poland in his time.

Derekh HaShem. Key work on Jewish thought by Rabbi Moshe Chaim Luzzatto (see *Adir BaMarom*), first printed in Amsterdam, 1896. Translated into English by Rabbi Aryeh Kaplan as *The Way of God* (Feldheim, New York, 1977).

Emunath Uman. Letters by Rabbi Nathan ben Reb Yehuda Reuven of Nemerov, (a leading disciple of Rabbi Nathan of Nemerov), and other Breslover leaders, edited by Rabbi Nathan Tzvi Koenig, and published in B'nei B'rak, 1966.

Etz Chaim. The major classic of Kabbalah, based on the teachings of the Ari (Rabbi Yitzchak Luria, 1534–1572), and written by Rabbi Chaim Vital (1542–1620), and first published in Koretz, 1782. Both the Ari, and his disciple Rabbi Chaim Vital, were the leaders of the Safed school of Kabbalah. Many consider the Ari to be the greatest of all Kabbalists.

Evven HaEzer. Third section of the *Shulchan Arukh* (q.v.) dealing with marriage and divorce.

Evven Shethiyah. Biographies of the Chasidic leaders of Kosov and Viznitz, by Rabbis Chaim Kahana and Chaim Yessachar Gross, published in Minkatch, 1930.

Eyn Yaakov. Collection of aggadoth (non-legal portions) of the Talmud, by Rabbi Yaakov (ben Shlomo) ibn Chabib (1433–1516), first published in Salonika, 1515–1522. We have used the Vilna, 1883, Romm edition, reprinted in New York, 1955.

Hagah. Gloss on the *Shulchan Arukh* (q.v.), presenting the Ashkenazic customs, by Rabbi Moshe (ben Yisrael) Isserles (1525–1572). Originally known as *HaMappah*, it was first published together with the *Shulchan Arukh* in Cracow, 1578, and in virtually every subsequent edition. The author was a leading rabbinical figure in Cracow, and one of the greatest halakhic authorities of all time.

HaGra. Commentary on *Shulchan Arukh* (q.v.) by Rabbi Eliahu (ben Shlomo, known as the Vilna Gaon (1720–1797), first printed with the *Shulchan Arukh* in Gorodna, 1806. The author was the greatest genius of his time, and the acknowledged leader of all non-Chassidic Jewry in Eastern Europe.

Handbook of Jewish Thought. Concise, encyclopedic work on basic Jewish theology, by Rabbi Aryeh Kaplan (Maznaim, Brooklyn, 1979).

Hekhaloth Rabathai. Important meditative work from the Merkava school of Kabbalah, attributed to Rabbi Yishmael (First Century), and also known as Pirkey Hekheloth. First printed as part of *Arzey Levanon,* Venice, 1601. We have used the edition published as part of *Batey Midrashoth* (q.v.), Volume 1, p. 67ff.

Idra Rabbah. Portion of the *Zohar* (q.v.) dealing with the dynamics of the supernal universes, presented as a lecture by Rabbi Shimon bar Yochai to his ten disciples. Found in the *Zohar* 3:127bff.

Idra Zutra. "The Lesser Gathering," so called because three of Rabbi Shimon's disciples had passed away. In the *Zohar* 3:287bff.

Karnayim. Kabbalistic work by Rabbi Aaron ben Avraham of Cordein, first published with commentary *Dan Yadin* (q.v.).

Kav HaYashar. Ethical classic by Rabbi Tzvi Hirsch (ben Aaron Shmuel) Kaidanover (1648–1712), first published in Frankfurt am Main, 1705. The author lived in Frankfurt.

Kedushath Shabbath. Breslover teachings regarding the Sabbath, by Rabbi Nachman (Goldstein) of Tcherin 1823–1898, published with *Yekara DeShabbatta,* Lemberg, 1876. The author was a student of Rabbi Nathan and a grandson of Rabbi Aharon, the Rabbi in Breslov during Rabbi Nachman's life.

Kehillath Yaakov. Dictionary of Kabbalistic terms, by Rabbi Yaakov Tzvi Yolles (died 1825), published in Lemberg, 1870. The author, who is best known for his *Maley Ro'im* on Talmudical concepts, was rabbi in Dinov.

Kohelleth Rabbah. Section of the *Midrash Rabbah* (q.v.) dealing with the book of Ecclesiastes.

Kokhavay Or. Stories and teachings of Rabbi Nachman and his disciples, by Rabbi Avraham ben Nachman of Tulchin (see Biur HaLikutim), first printed in Jerusalem, 1896. We have used the Jerusalem, 1972, edition.

Kramer, Rabbi Chaim. Oral teachings. Rabbi Kramer is the founder and director of the Breslov Research Institute and its affiliated *ba'alei teshuvah* and research institutes in Jerusalem.

Kramer, Rabbi Shmuel Moshe. Oral teachings, by a leading figure in Breslov in Jerusalem.

Light Beyond. Anthology of Chassidic philosophical teachings, divided according to subjects, by Rabbi Aryeh Kaplan (Maznaim, Brooklyn, 1981).

Likutey Etzoth B. See *Likutey Etzoth, Mahadura Bathra.*

Likutey Etzoth, Mahadura Bathra. Concise teachings and advice based on the works of Rabbi Nachman, by Rabbi Nachman of Tcherin, first published in Lemberg, 1874.

Likutey Halakhoth. Monumental work on Breslover thought and Kabbalah, following the order of the *Shulchan Arukh* (q.v.) by Rabbi Nathan of Nemerov, Rabbi Nachman's foremost disciple. First part printed in Jasse, 1843, with subsequent sections published through 1861. We have used the eight-volume, Jerusalem, 1970, edition.

Likutey Moharan. Primary work of Rabbi Nachman of Breslov, first printed in Ostrog, 1808, and in more than thirty subsequent editions. An ongoing translation with full annotation of this most important work is currently being rendered into English by the Breslov Research Institute. Since 1984, ten volumes out of fifteen are already completed.

Likutey Moharan Tinyana. The second part of *Likutey Moharan,* first printed in Mogolov, 1811. The two sections of *Likutey Moharan* were printed together in Breslov, 1821, and in all subsequent editions.

Likutey Torah. Kabbalistic Bible commentary based on the teachings of the Ari (see *Etz Chaim*) by Rabbi Chaim Vital, first printed in Zolkiev, 1775. We have used the Ashlag edition, Jerusalem, 1970.

Living Torah, The. A new translation of the *Five Books of Moses,* based on traditional Jewish sources, by Rabbi Aryeh Kaplan (Maznaim, Brooklyn, 1981).

The Lost Princess: And Other Kabbalistic Tales of Rebbe Nachman of Breslov (Woodstock, Vt.: Jewish Lights Publishing, 2005). The first twelve stories originally published by the Breslov Research Institute in *Rabbi Nachman's Stories.*

Maaseh Bitachon. Story #17, by Rabbi Nachman, first published by Rabbi Tzvi Dov ben Avraham of Berdichev, Jerusalem, 1905.

Maasiyoth U'Mashalim. Stories by Rabbi Nachman, preserved by his disciple, Rabbi Naftali of Nemerov, Uman, died 1809, printed as part of *Sippurim Niflaim* (q.v.), 1849 p. 14ff.

Maaver Yaavak. Laws and customs involving visiting the sick and funeral preparations, by Rabbi Aaron Berakhiah (ben Moshe) of Modina (died 1639), first printed in Venice, 1626. We have used the Zhitamar, 1852, edition, reprinted in B'nei B'rak, 1967. An important Kabbalist, the author lived in Italy.

Maggid Mesharim. Kabbalistic teachings given over by an angelic instructor (*maggid*) to Rabbi Yosef Caro (see *Shulchan Arukh*), first printed in Lublin, 1646, and completed in Venice, 1654. We have used the Jerusalem, 1960, edition.

MeAm Lo'ez. Monumental running commentary on the Torah, written in Ladino (Judeo-Spanish) by Rabbi Yaakov (ben Makhir) Culi (1689–1732), first published in Constantinople, 1730–1733. Upon the author's death, the set was completed by Rabbi Yitzchak (ben Moshe) Magriso and Rabbi Yitzchak Agruiti, as far as the portion of Ekev in Deuteronomy. A Hebrew translation, *Yalkut MeAm Lo'ez*, was completed by Rabbi Sh'muel Kreuser (Yerushalmi), Jerusalem, 1967–1971, and an English translation is being completed by Rabbi Aryeh Kaplan under the name of *The Torah Anthology* (q.v.). Rabbi Yaakov Culi was born in Jerusalem and later moved to Constantinople, where he was a leading figure in the Sephardic community.

Megaleh Amukoth. Kabbalistic interpretation of Moses' prayers by Rabbi Nathan Nateh (ben Shlomo) Spira (1585–1633), first published in Cracow, 1637. We have used the Furth, 1691, edition, reprinted in Brooklyn, 1975. The author was one of the foremost Kabbalists in Poland.

Mekhilta. The earliest commentary on the Book of Exodus, by the school of Rabbi Yishmael (circa 120 CE), often quoted in the Talmud. First printed in Constantinople, 1515.

Midbar Kedemoth. Alphabetical listing of important concepts, by Rabbi Chaim Yosef David Azzulai, known as the Chida (1724–1806), first printed in Lemberg, 1870. The author was one of the leading scholars and most prolific writers of his time.

Midrash Lekach Tov. Also known as *Pesikta Zutratha.* A Midrashic work by Rabbi Tovia (ben Eliezer) HaGadol (1036–1108), first printed in Venice, 1546. This work incorporates many earlier Midrashim that were circulating in fragmentary manuscripts. The author lived in Bulgaria and Serbia.

Midrash Rabbah. The most important collection of Midrashim, assembled during the early Gaonic period. The component Midrashim vary from almost pure commentary to pure homelies. All, however, are based on the teachings of the sages of the Talmud. The Midrash Rabbah on the Torah was first printed in Constantinople, 1512, while that on the five *megilloth* was printed in Pesaro, 1519.

Midrash Sh'muel. Commentary on *Avoth,* by Rabbi Shmuel (ben Yitzchak) Uceda (1538–1602), first printed in Venice, 1579. Often quoted by the *Tosefoth Yom Tov* (q.v.). The author studied Kabbalah under the Ari and Rabbi Chaim Vital (see *Etz Chaim*). He established a major yeshiva in Safed where both Talmud and Kabbalah were taught.

Midrash Shochar Tov. See *Midrash Tehillim.*

Midrash Tehillim. Also known as *Midrash Shochar Tov.* An ancient Midrash on the Psalms, first printed in Constantinople, 1515. A critical edition, based on manuscript, was published by Shlomo Buber, Vilna, 1891.

Nachaley Emunah. Letters of Rabbi Nachman of Tulchin (the foremost student of Rabbi Nathan of Nemerov) and other Breslover leaders, edited by Rabbi Nathan Tzvi Koenig, first printed in B'nei B'rak, 1967.

Nachath HaShulchan. Work on the *Shulchan Arukh* (q.v.) based on the first lesson of *Likutey Moharan* (q.v.), by Rabbi Nachman of Tcherin, first published in Jerusalem, 1910. We have used the Jerusalem, 1968, edition.

Nevey Tzaddikim. Historical bibliography of all Breslover works, by Rabbi Nathan Tzvi Koenig, published in B'nei B'rak, 1969.

Oneg Shabbath. Collections of letters and lessons explaining Breslover teachings, by Rabbi Ephraim Tzvi (ben Alter Ben-Tzion) Krakavski of Pshedbarz (1880–1946), published in New York, 1966.

Or HaGanuz. Commentary on the *Bahir* (q.v.) by Rabbi Meir ben Shalom Abi-Sahula, written in 1331 and published anonymously in Vilna, 1883, together with the *Bahir.* The author was a student of the Rashba (q.v.).

Orach Chaim. First section of the *Shulchan Arukh* (q.v.) dealing with prayers and holy days.

Othioth deRabbi Akiva. Commentary on the letters of the Hebrew alphabet, attributed to Rabbi Akiva (circa 100 CE), first published in Constantinople, 1516. We have used the version in *Batey Midrashoth* (q.v.).

Pardes Rimonim. Major Kabbalistic work by Rabbi Moshe Cordovero (1522–1570), first published in Salonica, 1583. The author was the head of the Safed school of Kabbalah before the Ari (see *Etz Chaim*).

Parparoth LeChokhmah. Major commentary on *Likutey Moharan* (q.v.) by Rabbi Nachman of Tcherin, first published in Lemberg, 1876.

Peney Moshe. Standard commentary on the *Yerushalmi* (q.v.) by Rabbi Meir (ben Shimon) Margolioth (died 1781), first published in Amsterdam, 1754. Printed together with most editions of the *Yerushalmi.*

Pirkey deRabbi Eliezer. Important Midrashic work by the school of Rabbi Eliezer (ben Hyrcanos) HaGadol (circa 100 CE), first published in Constantinople, 1514. We have used the Warsaw, 1852 edition, which includes a commentary by Rabbi David Luria, the Radal.

Pri Etz Chaim. Important Kabbalistic work on meditations for various prayers and rituals, based on the teachings of the Ari (see *Etz Chaim*), by Rabbi Chaim Vital, first published in Koretz, 1782.

Rabbi Nachman's Wisdom. Translation of *Shevachey HaRan* and *Sichoth HaRan* (q.v.) by Rabbi Aryeh Kaplan, published in New York, 1973.

Ramban. Acronym of Rabbi Moshe ben Nachman (1194–1270), denoting his commentary on the Torah, first printed in Rome, 1472. The author was a leading spiritual leader of his time, writing over fifty major works. He maintained a yeshiva in Gerona, Spain.

Rashba. Acronym of Rabbi Shimon ben Avraham Adret (1235–1310). His commentaries on the aggadoth of the Talmud were published together with *Eyn Yaakov* (q.v.) in Salonika, 1515. A student of the Ramban (q.v.), the author was rabbi of Barcelona and one of the major Jewish leaders of his time.

Rashi. Acronym of Rabbi Shlomo (ben Yitzchak) Yarchi (see Shem HaGedolim) or Yitzchaki (1040–1105), author of the most important commentaries on the Bible and Talmud, printed in almost all major editions. His commentary on the Torah was the first known Hebrew book to be published (Rome, circa 1470). He headed yeshivoth in Troyes, France, and Worms, Germany. His commentaries are renowned for being extremely terse, immediately bringing forth the main idea of the text.

Recanti. Torah commentary of Rabbi Menachem (ben Binyamin) Recanti (1210–1305), first published in Venice, 1523. We have used the edition with the commentary of Rabbi Mordechai Yaffe, Lemberg, 1880. The author was one of the leading Kabbalists of his time, and the first to quote the *Zohar* (q.v.).

Reshith Chokhmah. An encyclopedic work on morality (*mussar*), drawing heavily on the *Zohar* (q.v.) by Rabbi Eliahu (ben Moshe) de Vidas (1518–1592), first published in Venice, 1579. A student of Rabbi Moshe Cordovero (see *Pardes Rimonim*), the author had a reputation as a sage and saint.

Rimzey Maasioth. Commentaries on the Stories, by Rabbi Nachman of Tcherin. First printed in Lemberg, 1902, and with all subsequent editions of the Stories.

Rimzey Maasioth, Hashmatoth. Additional commentaries on the Stories by Rabbi Abraham ben Nachman of Tulchin, printed in the Lemberg, 1902, edition of *Sippurey Maasioth*.

Rokeach. An important code of Jewish law and pietistic practice by Rabbi Eleazar (ben Yehudah) Rokeach of Worms (1164–1232), first printed in Fano, 1505. Besides being a leading authority in Jewish law, the author was one of the foremost masters of Kabbalah in his time.

Rosenfeld, Rabbi Tzvi Aryeh Benzion (ben Yisrael Abba) (1922–1978). A descendant of Rabbi Aaron, rabbi in Breslov in the time of Rabbi Nachman, and of Rabbi Shmuel Yitzchok of Tcherin, one of Rabbi Nachman's leading disciples, Rabbi Rosenfeld was one of the leaders of Breslover Chasidim in America. He left numerous tapes of lectures and lessons on the Stories, as well as handwritten marginal notes on his private copy of *Sippurey Maasioth,* now in the hands of his son-in-law, Rabbi Noson Maimon.

Sefer Baal Shem Tov. Anthology of writings of the Baal Shem Tov (1698–1760), founder of the Chasidic movement, by Rabbi Shimon Mendel Vidnik of Givarchav, first published in Lodz, 1938.

Sefer Chasidim. Laws and customs of the Chasidey Ashkenaz (German Pietists) by Rabbi Yehudah (ben Shmuel) HaChasid (1148–1217), first printed in Bologna,

1538. The author, who lived in Speyer and Regensberg, was a master Kabbalist, and a leading rabbinical authority.

Sefer HaMiddoth. Alphabetical listing of concise practical lessons, by Rabbi Nachman of Breslov, first published in Mogolov, 1811.

Sefer HaPeliah. Kabbalistic classic, also known as *Sefer HaKanah,* attributed to the school of Rabbi Nechunia ben Hakana (see *Bahir*). Thought to have been written by Rabbi Elkana ben Yerocham, first published in Koretz, 1784.

Sefer Tekhunah. Astronomical work by Rabbi Chaim Vital (see *Etz Chaim*), first published in Jerusalem, 1866. We have used the Jerusalem, 1967, edition.

Sefer Yetzirah. One of the earliest and most important mystical works, thought to have been written in Talmudic times or earlier. There are some who attribute the authorship to Abraham. First printed in Mantua, 1562, it has been the subject of over a hundred commentaries.

Sefer Zerubavel. Ancient eschatological work, first printed in Constantinople, 1524, and in *Batey Midrashoth* (q.v.), Volume 2, p. 495ff. Probably written in late Talmudic times, it was used by Saadia Gaon (882–942 CE).

Shaar HaGilgulim. A detailed work on reincarnation, the last of the "Eight Gates" (*Shemonah Shaarim*) based on the Kabbalah of the Ari, by Rabbi Chaim Vital, first published in Jerusalem, 1863. We have used the Ashlag edition, Tel Aviv, 1963.

Shaar HaKavanoth. Kabbalistic meditations on the worship service and rituals, the sixth of the "Eight Gates," by Rabbi Chaim Vital, first published in Salonika, 1852. We have used the Ashlag edition, Tel Aviv, 1962.

Shaar HaMitzvoth. Kabbalistic interpretations of the commandments, the fifth of the "Eight Gates," by Rabbi Chaim Vital, first published in Salonika, 1852. We have used the Ashlag edition, Tel Aviv, 1962.

Shaar Ruach HaKodesh. Meditative methods, the seventh of the "Eight Gates," by Rabbi Chaim Vital, first published in Jerusalem, 1863. We have used the Ashlag edition, Tel Aviv, 1963.

Shaarey Orah. Major Kabbalah classic, by Rabbi Yosef (ben Avraham) Gikatilla

(1248–1345), first printed in Riva de Trento, 1561. The author, who lived in Italy, was a student of Rabbi Avraham Abulafia.

Shaarey Tzion. Important collection of Kabbalistic prayers, by Rabbi Nathan Nata (ben Moshe) Hanover (died 1683), first published in Prague, 1662. The author was a leading Kabbalist.

Shaarey Zohar. Index and commentary of the Talmud, cross-referenced to the *Zohar,* by Rabbi Reuven Margoliot (1889–1971), published in Jerusalem, 1956.

She'erith Yisrael. Collection of letters by the elders of Breslov, edited by Rabbi Nathan Tzvi Koenig, published in B'nei B'rak, 1963.

Shefa Tal. Important Kabbalistic work by Rabbi Shabathai Sheftel (ben Akiva HaLevi) Horowitz (1561–1619), first published in Hanau, 1612.

Shemoth Rabbah. Section of the *Midrash Rabbah* (q.v.) dealing with the Book of Exodus.

Shir HaShirim Rabbah. Section of the *Midrash Rabbah* (q.v.) dealing with the Song of Songs.

Shiur Komah. Book of Kabbalistic concepts by Rabbi Moshe Cordovero (see *Pardes Rimonim*), published in Warsaw, 1883.

Shivechey HaRan. Highlights of Rabbi Nachman's life, including his pilgrimage to the Holy Land, by Rabbi Nathan of Nemerov, first published in Ostrog, 1816. Translated into English as part of *Rabbi Nachman's Wisdom* (q.v.). Parts are included in the *Gems of Rabbi Nachman,* by Rabbi Aryeh Kaplan, New York, 1980.

Shivechey Moharan. Anecdotes and teachings of Rabbi Nachman, compiled by Rabbi Nathan of Nemerov, printed together with *Chayay Moharan* (q.v.).

Shulchan Arukh. The standard code of Jewish Law, by Rabbi Yosef (ben Ephraim) Caro (1488–1575), first published in Venice, 1564. Divided into four parts, *Orach Chaim, Yoreh Deah, Evven HaEzer,* and *Choshen Mishpat.* Born in Spain, the author migrated to Turkey after the expulsion in 1492, and then to Safed, where he served as chief rabbi. With the addition of the *Hagah* (q.v.), the *Shulchan Arukh* became the standard work on Jewish Law for all Jewry.

Sichoth HaRan. Short teachings and sayings of Rabbi Nachman of Breslov, collected by Rabbi Nathan of Nemerov, first published together with *Sippurey Maasioth*, Ostrog, 1816. An expanded edition, including much new material, was published in Zolkiev, 1850. Translated into English as part of *Rabbi Nachman's Wisdom* (q.v.). Selections are included in *Gems of Rabbi Nachman* by Rabbi Aryeh Kaplan, New York, 1980.

Sichoth VeSippurim. Exposition of Rabbi Nachman's teachings, including commentary on the Stories, by Rabbi Avraham ben Nachman of Tulchin, published in Jerusalem, 1913. Reprinted as part of *Kokhavey Or* (q.v.).

Sifethey Cohen. Commentary on *Yoreh Deah* and *Choshen Mishpat* (q.v.) by Rabbi Shabethai (ben Meir) HaCohen (1621–1662), usually referred to as the Shakh. First published alone in Cracow, 1646, and later with most standard editions of the *Shulchan Arukh* (q.v.).

Sippurey Maasioth. The Stories of Rabbi Nachman, translated here in this volume. First published in Ostrog, 1816, and with a new introduction, in Lemberg, 1850.

Sippurim Niflaim. Anecdotes and teachings involving Rabbi Nachman of Breslov, as well as previously unpublished stories, collected by Rabbi Shmuel Horowitz (1903–1973). First published in Jerusalem in 1935.

Sternhartz, Rabbi Avraham (ben Reb Naftali Hertz) (1862–1955). A great-grandson of Rabbi Nathan, and grandson of Rabbi Nachman of Tcherin, he was one of the most important elders of Breslov in Uman, USSR and Jerusalem. Among his many students were Rabbi Tzvi Aryeh Rosenfeld (q.v.), Rabbi Gedaliah Koenig, and Rabbi Nachman Burstyn who included many of his teachings in his lectures (see *Tovoth Zikhronoth*).

Talmud. The embodiment of the Oral Torah, as taught by the great masters from approximately 50 BCE until around 500 CE. The first part to be codified was the Mishnah, set in its present form by Rabbi Yehudah the Prince, around 188 CE. Subsequent discussions were redacted as the Gemara by Rav Ashi and Ravina in Babylonia around 505 CE, and it is therefore often referred to as the Babylonian Talmud. Next to the Bible itself, it is the most important work on Jewish law and theology. Individual volumes of the Talmud were printed in Soncino, Italy, as early as 1482, but the entire Talmud was first printed by David Bomberg in Venice, 1523, along with the commentaries of Rashi and Tosafoth (q.v.). (Also see *Yerushalmi.*)

Tana deBei Eliahu Rabba and Zuta. An early Midrash attributed to the teachings of the prophet Elijah, first printed in Venice, 1598.

Tanchuma. An early homiletic Midrash on the Torah, attributed to Rabbi Tanchuma bar Abba (circa 370 CE), but added to until around 850 CE. First printed in Constantinople, 1522.

Targum. Authorized Aramaic translation of the Torah, by the proselyte Onkelos (around 90 CE). In Talmudic times, it was read along with the Torah, so that the congregation could understand the reading.

Targum Yonathan. Aramaic translation of the Torah, attributed to Yonathan ben Uzziel (circa 50 CE). Portions appear to have been amended in Gaonic times.

Tifereth Yisrael. Theological work, discussing the significance of Israel and the Torah, by Rabbi Yehudah (ben Betzalel) Loew (1424–1609), first published in Venice, 1599. The author, known as the Maharal of Prague, was one of the most respected rabbis of his time, and is credited with having made the Golem.

Tikkun HaKelali. The Ten Psalms prescribed by Rabbi Nachman as a "General Rectification" for sexual and other sins, first published by Rabbi Nathan of Nemerov, Breslov, 1821. Available in English as "Rabbi Nachman's Tikun," published by the Breslov Research Institute, 1982.

Tikkuney Zohar. Part of the Zoharic literature, consisting of seventy chapters on the first word of the Torah, by the school of Rabbi Shimon bar Yochai (circa 120 CE), first printed in Mantua, 1558. However, a second edition, *Orto Koy,* 1719, provided the basis for all subsequent editions. The work contains some of the most important discussions in Kabbalah and is essential for understanding the system of the *Zohar* (q.v.).

Tikkuney Zohar Chadash. Additions to the *Zohar Chadash* (q.v.) in the manner of *Tikkuney Zohar.*

Toledoth Yaakov Yosef. The first Chassidic work, by Rabbi Yaakov Yosef of Polonoye (died 1782), first published in Koretz, 1780. The author was the senior disciple of the Baal Shem Tov, founder of Chasidism.

Torah Anthology, The. Translation of *MeAm Lo'ez* (q.v.) by Rabbi Aryeh Kaplan.

Tosafoth. Collection of commentaries, using Talmudic methodology on the Talmud itself. The work was a product of the yeshiva academies of France and Germany between around 1100 and 1300, begun by the students of Rashi (q.v.) and his grandsons, most notably, Rabbi Yaakov Tam (circa 1100–1171). It is printed in virtually all editions of the Talmud.

Tosefoth Yom Tov. Important commentary on the Mishnah (see Talmud) by Rabbi Yom Tov Lipman (ben Nathan HaLevi) Heller (1579–1654), first published in Prague, 1614–1617). The author, who served as rabbi in Prague and Poland, was a student of the Maharal (see *Tifereth Yisrael*).

Tosefta. Additions to the Mishnah (see Talmud) by Rabbis Chiya and Oshia (circa 230 CE), published together with most editions of the Talmud. The *Tosefta* is often quoted in the Talmud itself. We have used the paragraphing found in the Romm edition of the Talmud, Vilna, 1880–1886.

Tovoth Zikhronoth. Breslover traditions, by Rabbi Avraham (ben Naftali Hertz) Sternhartz (Kokhav Lev) (1862–1955), published in Jerusalem, 1951. The author was one of the Breslover elders in Jerusalem.

VaYakhel Moshe. Important Kabbalistic work by Rabbi Moshe (ben Menachem) Graff of Prague (1650–1707), first printed in Dessau, 1699.

VaYikra Rabbah. Section of the *Midrash Rabbah* (q.v.) on the Book of Leviticus.

Yad. Short for *Yad Chazakah,* otherwise known as *Mishneh Torah,* the monumental Code of Jewish Law by Rabbi Moshe ben Maimonides (1135–1204), better known as the Rambam. The work was so named because of its fourteen divisions, the numerical value of *Yad.* It was the first systematic codification of Jewish law, and the only one that encompasses every aspect of the Torah. Considered one of the great classics of Torah literature, it was first printed in Rome, 1475. It has been printed in many editions and is the subject of dozens of commentaries.

Yagel Yaakov. Collection of letters and lessons on Breslov teachings, by Rabbi Yaakov Gedaliah (ben Nethanel) Tefilinsky (1941–1971), published by Rabbi

Nathan Tzvi Koenig, B'nei B'rak, 1972.

Yalkut Shimoni. Also known as the Yalkut, one of the most popular early Midrashic collections on the Bible, compiled by Rabbi Shimon Ashkenazi HaDarshan of Frankfort (circa 1260), first printed in Salonika, 1521–1527. Many Midrashim are known only because they are cited in this work. The author was a preacher in Frankfort.

Yemey Moharnat. Biography of Rabbi Nathan of Nemerov. The first section was printed in Lemberg, 1876, and the second part, dealing with Rabbi Nathan's pilgrimage to the Land of Israel, was printed in Jerusalem, 1904. A full biography, *Through Fire and Water: The Life of Reb Noson of Breslov,* is available in English from the Breslov Research Institute, 1991.

Yerach HaEthanim. Breslover teachings about the power of a Tzaddik, Rosh Hashana, Yom Kippur, and Succoth based on *Likutey Moharan,* by Rabbi Nachman of Tcherin, published in Jerusalem, 1951.

Yerioth Sh'lomo. Monumental work on Hebrew synonyms and language, by Rabbi Shlomo (ben Zelligman) Pappenhiem (1760–1840), in three parts, published in Dyherenfurth, 1784, 1811, Roedelheim, 1831. The work is often quoted (as the Rashap) in *HaKethav VeHaKabbalah* and is said to have influenced Rabbi Shimshon Raphael Hirsch. The author served as a *dayyan* (rabbinical judge) in Breslau.

Yerushalmi. Or *Talmud Yerushalmi.* An earlier version of the Talmud, thought to have been redacted around 240 CE by Rabbi Yochanan (182–279 CE) and his disciples in Tiberias with the concurrence of the sages of Jerusalem. A work of major importance, although considered secondary to the Babylonian Talmud. It was first published in Venice, 1523. We have used the Romm, Vilna, 1922–1928, edition.

Yoreh Deah. Second section of the *Shulchan Arukh* (q.v.), dealing with dietary laws and other areas requiring rabbinical decision.

Zera Berakh. Torah commentary by Rabbi Berakhia Berakh (ben Yitzchak) Spira (1598–1666), published in Cracow, 1646, with additions in Amsterdam, 1662. The author was a son-in-law of Rabbi Yom Tov Lipman Heller (see *Tosefoth Yom Tov*) and served as preacher and *dayyan* (rabbinical judge) in Cracow.

Zimrath HaAretz. Breslover teachings regarding the importance of the Land of Israel, by Rabbi Nachman of Tcherin, published in Lemberg, 1876. We have used the Jerusalem, 1968, edition.

Zohar. The primary classic of Kabbalah, from the school of Rabbi Shimon bar Yochai (circa 120 CE), compiled by his disciple, Rabbi Abba. After being restricted to a small, closed circle of Kabbalists and hidden for centuries, it was finally published around 1290 by Rabbi Moshe (ben Shem Tov) de Leon (1239–1305). After considerable controversy, Rabbi Yitzchak Yehoshua (ben Yaakov Bonet) de Lattes (1498–1571) issued an opinion that it was permitted to print the *Zohar,* and it was published in Mantua, 1558–1560. It has been reprinted in over sixty subsequent editions and is the subject of dozens of commentaries.

Zohar Chadash. The "New *Zohar,*" by the school of Rabbi Shimon bar Yochai, consisting of manuscripts found in the possession of the Safed Kabbalists, assembled by Rabbi Avraham (ben Eliezer HaLevi) Barukhim (1516–1593), and printed in Salonika, 1597. It was called the "New *Zohar*" because it was printed after the original *Zohar.*

Zohar HaRakia. Commentary on the *Zohar* by the Ari (see *Etz Chaim*), and edited by Rabbi Yaakov Tzemach, first published in Koretz, 1785.

ABOUT THE BRESLOV RESEARCH INSTITUTE

Rebbe Nachman was only 38 years old when he passed away in 1810. Yet, shortly before his passing, he told his followers that his influence would endure long afterwards. "My light will burn until the days of the Mashiach [Messiah]." Generations of readers have been enthralled and inspired by his writings, which have been explored and interpreted by leading scholars around the globe.

The growing interest in Rebbe Nachman from all sectors—academia and laymen alike—led to the establishment of the Breslov Research Institute in Jerusalem in 1979. Since then a team of scholars has been engaged in research into the texts, oral traditions and music of the Breslov movement. The purpose of the Institute is to publish authoritative translations, commentaries and general works on Breslov Chassidut. Projects also include the recording of Breslov songs and melodies on cassette and in music book form.

Offices and representatives of the Breslov Research Institute:

Israel:

Breslov Research Institute
P.O. Box 5370
Jerusalem, Israel
Tel: (011-9722) 582-4641
Fax: (011-9722) 582-5542
www.breslov.org

North America:
Breslov Research Institute
P.O. Box 587
Monsey, NY 10952-0587
Tel: (845) 425-4258
Fax: (845) 425-3018
www.breslov.org

Breslov books may be ordered directly from these offices.

BRESLOV RESEARCH INSTITUTE BOOKS

Rabbi Nachman's Stories

Translated by *Rabbi Aryeh Kaplan*

The Sages always told stories to convey some of the deepest secrets about God and His relation to the creation. Rebbe Nachman developed this ancient art to perfection. Spellbinding and entertaining, these stories are fast moving, richly structured and filled with penetrating insights. Rabbi Kaplan's translation is accompanied by a masterful commentary drawn from the works of Rebbe Nachman's chassidim.

6 x 9, 552 pages, HC, Bibliography, Index, ISBN 0-930213-02-5

Crossing the Narrow Bridge
A Practical Guide to Rebbe Nachman's Teachings

by *Chaim Kramer;* ed. by *Moshe Mykoff*

Rebbe Nachman taught: "The world is a very narrow bridge. The main thing is not to be afraid." Lively, down to earth and easy to read, this book provides clear, detailed guidance in how to apply Rebbe Nachman's teachings in modern everyday life. Subjects include faith, joy, meditating, earning a living, health, raising children, etc., and provide a wealth of anecdotes from the lives of leading Breslov chassidim.

5½ x 8½, 452 pages, HC, Appendices, ISBN 0-930213-40-8

The Breslov Haggadah

Compiled and translated by *Rabbi Yehoshua Starret* and *Chaim Kramer;* ed. by *Moshe Mykoff*

The classic Pesach Haggadah accompanied by Rebbe Nachman's unique insights and other commentary material drawn from Breslov and general sources. Includes appendices on: The Story of Exodus, Pesach Anecdotes, Chassidic insights into *Sefirat HaOmer, Chol HaMoed,* and *Shavuot.* 6½ x 9½, 256 pages, HC, Appendices, ISBN 0-930213-35-1

Esther: *A Breslov Commentary on the Megillah*
Compiled and adapted by *Rabbi Yehoshua Starret;* ed. by *Ozer Bergman*
Insights from Rebbe Nachman and his followers that "unmask" the Megillah's deeper meaning in the modern context and for each of us personally. Includes Hebrew text of the Megillah, laws of the holiday and historical overview.
6 x 8½, 160 pages, PB, Appendices, ISBN 0-930213-42-4

Chanukah—*With Rebbe Nachman of Breslov*
Compiled and adapted by *Rabbi Yehoshua Starret*
Traces the historical roots—and spiritual implications—of the Chanukah story, and provides deeper insight into the holiday's laws and their meaning for today. Based on the timeless wisdom of Rebbe Nachman and other Chassidic masters, this work lights the way on the journey from ancient Israel to the future, and into the mind and heart.
5 x 8, 128 pages, PB, ISBN 0-930213-99-8

Garden of the Souls: *Rebbe Nachman on Suffering*
by *Avraham Greenbaum*
Offers guidance and comfort in dealing with pain and suffering in our own lives and those of the people around us. Faith makes it possible to find meaning in the trials of this world and turn them into experiences that can elevate us spiritually and open us to profound joy.
5 x 8, 96 pages, PB, ISBN 0-930213-39-4

Anatomy of the Soul
by *Chaim Kramer;* ed. by *Avraham Sutton*
Explores the mystical meaning of the teaching that human beings are created in the image of God; provides an in-depth study of how the different systems of the human body relate to the ten *sefirot* and the five levels of the soul, and how through the body's organs and limbs we influence the hidden spiritual universes.
6 x 9, 364 pages, HC, Appendices, ISBN 0-930213-51-3

Rabbi Nachman's Wisdom
Translated by *Rabbi Aryeh Kaplan;* ed. by *Rabbi Zvi Aryeh Rosenfeld*
A classic collection of Rebbe Nachman's conversations and teachings, ranging from comments on everyday practical topics to fundamental insights about faith and Jewish mysticism. The conversations provide a vivid picture of the Master, his wit, directness and wisdom. Also included is an account of Rebbe Nachman's adventure-filled pilgrimage to the Holy Land at the height of Napoleon's campaign in the Middle East in 1798.
6 x 9, 486 pages, HC, Appendices, Index, ISBN 0-930213-00-9

Likutey Moharan: *The Collected Teachings of Rabbi Nachman*
Translated by *Moshe Mykoff;* annotated by *Chaim Kramer*
The first authoritative translation of Rebbe Nachman's *magnum opus,* presented with facing punctuated Hebrew text, full explanatory notes, source references and supplementary information relating to the lessons. Each volume is accompanied by appendices and charts clarifying pertinent kabbalistic concepts; the first volume includes Reb Noson's introduction to the original work, short biographies of leading Breslov personalities and a bibliography.
Vol. 1—*Lessons 1–6:* 6½ x 9½, HC, ISBN 0-930213-92-0
Vol. 2—*Lessons 7–16:* 6½ x 9½, HC, ISBN 0-930213-93-9
Vol. 3—*Lessons 17–22:* 6½ x 9½, HC, ISBN 0-930213-78-5
Vol. 4—*Lessons 23–32:* 6½ x 9½, HC, ISBN 0-930213-79-3
Vol. 5—*Lessons 33–48:* 6½ x 9½, HC, ISBN 0-930213-80-7
Vol. 6—*Lessons 49–57:* 6½ x 9½, HC, ISBN 0-930213-81-5
Vol. 7—*Lessons 58–64:* 6½ x 9½, HC, ISBN 0-930213-82-3
Vol. 10—*Lessons 109–194:* 6½ x 9½, HC, ISBN 0-930213-85-8
Vol. 11—*Lessons 195–286:* 6½ x 9½, HC, ISBN 0-930213-86-6